HOW TO

Write a Manual

Elizabeth Slatkin

TEN SPEED PRESS
BERKELEY, CALIFORNIA

Acknowledgments

I would like to thank my editor, Mariah Bear, for her help, encouragement, and most of all for her insightful critique of my work.

For all those who have attended one of my seminars, thank you for your comments, suggestions, questions, real-world applications and problems. I have enjoyed our discussions and learned a great deal.

And to Bruce Dawson, who looked over the material I was using in my seminar on writing user manuals and said: "You ought to publish this."

1❧

Ten Speed Press
P.O. Box 7123
Berkeley, CA 94707

First Printing 1991

Cover design by Fifth Street Design
Text design by Sarah Levin
Typesetting by Wilsted & Taylor

Library of Congress Cataloging-in-Publication Data

Slatkin, Elizabeth.
    How to write a manual / Elizabeth Slatkin.
        p.   cm.
    Includes bibliographical references and index.
    ISBN 0-89815-430-8
    1. Technical writing.   2. Technical manuals.   I. Title.
T11.S55   1991
808'.0666—dc20   91-4795
                                                    CIP

Printed in the United States of America
1   2   3   4   5–95   94   93   92   91

Table of Contents

List of Figures

GETTING STARTED

What Is this Book About?

This book shows you how to write a user manual. It provides you with tools to use in thinking your way through large, complex writing projects in the workplace, and offers practical guidelines for structuring and controlling such projects, from start to finish.

This book teaches a structured approach to problem solving. By this I mean that groups of questions lead you through the process of creating a manual that meets project requirements. Knowing the right questions to ask will allow you to create high-quality manuals for a variety of projects.

Among the examples in this book, the software user manual is most frequently mentioned. Why?

One, more and more products are based on complex technology, especially software. Customers often find it difficult to understand and use such products. Therefore, user manuals for such products play an important role in making them truly usable. If the manual is well written, it adds value by improving customer satisfaction with your products.

Two, many companies invest large amounts of time and money in developing software user manuals for staff as well as customers, because computers are used for so many specialized tasks. Even companies whose primary business is not the development and marketing of software create many of these manuals: aircraft builders, credit card companies, banks, telephone companies, shoe companies, and so on.

Three, the writing of a software user manual is a large, complex project that involves many people from many departments—a rich opportunity for problems and conflict, unless the project is properly handled.

Why a Book About "How to Write a Manual"?

Business surveys and my own experience in teaching seminars on this subject indicate that writing manuals is one of the most common on-the-job tasks, second only to writing letters and memos. Surprised? Well, consider . . .

Manuals tell us how to assemble, use, maintain, and repair all sorts of products. Manuals also specify company operating procedures, describe jobs, provide information for staff, and explain how to train employees. People come and go, and we need permanent "memory banks" to ensure smooth business operations and ongoing productivity.

While hypertext, hypermedia, and other online interfaces will some-day allow products to talk and demonstrate and explain and repair them-selves, right now written manuals *on paper* are the principal means of com-munication for teaching and learning.

My clients and seminar attendees ask these questions again and again:

> *What are the problems in organizing a project to create a user manual, and how can I avoid them?*
>
> *Is there a practical, effective method for creating a user manual that meets project requirements and gets the job done?*

And that is why I wrote this book.

Who Should Read this Book?

Do you need a book that does not assume previous knowledge or experi-ence in developing manuals?

Do you need a practical, easy-to-use approach that is structured and task oriented?

Do you need a book that will help you sharpen your thinking and writ-ing skills, while recognizing that most people are not professional writers?

Are you the manager of a communications group who has been search-ing for a way to coordinate your project team's efforts?

Would you like all your company's manuals to be consistent in orga-nization and appearance?

Are you an engineer, systems analyst, or product developer who needs to work with documentation specialists, technical writers, or other professional communicators, and to understand their perspectives?

Are you an information executive who would like to learn how your company could create better manuals in a more cost/time-efficient framework?

Are you a professional business or technical writer who would appreciate a book that cuts through the theory and provides proven techniques for your projects?

This book is for you if you work in business, industry, science, or government and wish to develop your ability to communicate effectively. It is intended for managers, information executives, scientists, engineers, product developers, systems analysts, consultants, professional communicators, and others who wish to learn methods for creating superior user manuals.

How Will You Benefit from Reading this Book?

You will learn practical techniques for creating better user manuals. Specifically, you will learn how to:

- Plan a manual-development project in a work environment.
- Ask the key questions that will determine the project's success.
- Define your audience and its needs.
- Accommodate different audiences in one manual.
- Ask the right conceptual and design questions.
- Use the most helpful page and text formatting styles.
- Understand the purpose and use of an outline.
- Understand structural styles and how to select one for an outline.
- Conduct information-gathering interviews with product experts.
- Understand the basic principles of good writing style.
- Control the first draft and revisions.
- Evaluate the manual according to initial project requirements.
- Decide when the manual is finished.
- Provide quality-control checks throughout the project.

How Is this Book Organized?

A *Table of Contents* and a *List of Figures* at the beginning of the book help you find information. The Table of Contents shows the "big picture," or "road map"; skim it to see where you'll be going in your journey through the text.

Chapter 1, *Why Are Manuals Important?*, shows you how user manuals fit into the business communication system.

Chapter 2, *Here's Your Road Map*, serves two purposes: First, it describes the organization of the rest of this book. In addition, as the book itself is, in fact, a user manual for writers of user manuals, chapter 2 doubles as a road map to guide you through projects.

Chapters 3 through 9, *Planning* through *Evaluating Your Manual*, take you step-by-step through the process of creating a user manual, following the road map presented in chapter 2.

Chapter 10, *Production*, offers suggestions and rules of thumb for producing copies of your original manual.

Chapter 11, *Exercises*, offers real-world scenarios for practicing what you learn in this book.

An *Index* at the end will help you quickly find topics of interest. This is especially useful once you have read the book and need to refer to it during a project.

How Should You Use this Book?

This book is primarily intended as a series of hands-on, step-by-step lessons. If you have little or no manual-writing experience, you will benefit most from reading the entire book before you start a project.

If you have some experience, or are a professional communicator, use the table of contents, list of figures, and index to jump quickly to topics of interest.

1

WHY ARE MANUALS IMPORTANT?

Manuals are important because *knowledge doesn't do anybody any good unless it is effectively transmitted and acquired.*

As we face the challenges of living in the Information Age, with new knowledge generated at an ever-increasing rate, we must become much better at transmitting and acquiring knowledge.

The demand to understand a product, a process, or a subject is part of our lives. We need to bridge the gap between what we know and what we must learn in order to achieve our personal and professional goals.

A product doesn't do users any good unless they can understand how to use it to get a job done. And the faster that knowledge can be communicated, the better the product performs and the greater its potential for success in the marketplace. A product truly exists only to the degree to which users perceive how and why it is useful, *and* that it is easy to use.

Manuals are a major channel for transmitting information and instructions about products to users. If companies intend to "mainstream" products based on new and complex technologies, they must focus on *human factors* such as ease of use, clear instructions, and effective training for their audiences. Good user manuals take a *human factors approach,* and often must compensate for the lack of such an approach in the product itself.

It is a question of perspective. The following figure shows the difference between a product-development and a product-communication perspective. Both are necessary for success, but the developer and the communicator are not usually the same person.

Developer	Communicator
Product oriented	User oriented
Views technology as end in itself	Views technology as means to an end
Interested in how to create the product and make it work	Interested in why the product would be created and how it could be used
Interested in features and functions, methods of operating product	Interested in applying product's features, functions, and operations to solving problems
Product expert	User expert
Skilled in creating product	Skilled in communicating product

Fig. 1: Developer and Communicator Perspectives

Bad User Manuals Are Not Productive

A *good* user manual keeps user overhead to a minimum. Why is that important? And what are some of the hidden costs of *bad* user manuals?

When users first pick up one of your manuals, how do they feel about it? Do they have to search for information, flipping pages and wondering where the table of contents or index is? Do they have to spend time trying to figure out what your acronyms, abbreviations, terms, and symbols mean? Do they have to deal with out-of-order steps in instructions? Look for figures that are not numbered, referenced, or near the accompanying text? Can they actually use it to accomplish a task easily and quickly with minimal frustration? Is your manual truly usable?

Good User Manuals Mean Business

Manuals are everywhere in business, industry, science, and government. According to the *Wall Street Journal* (6/21/85: "Technical Manual Produc-

- ✔ Endless searches for procedural information
- ✔ Calls to the product vendor or manufacturer
- ✔ Trips to the retailer
- ✔ Ongoing training workshops
- ✔ Consultants
- ✔ Continual self-teaching, with no sense of learning or accomplishment
- ✔ Much frustration
- ✔ Downtime caused by lengthy installations and adjustments
- ✔ High learning curves
- ✔ Ongoing opportunity costs and lost business
- ✔ Lower productivity
- ✔ Negative impact on the bottom line
- ✔ The job for which the product was purchased does not get done

Fig. 2: Hidden Costs of Bad User Manuals

tion Finally Enters Computer Age"), the Navy alone has about 200,000 manuals which are constantly being revised.

Many companies resist investing time and money in creating good user manuals, because they do not understand the hidden costs of bad ones. To be successful, a product must not only *be* easy to use, it must appear that way to your customer. With good user manuals:

- *Your products will be easier to sell* because the manual will show customers how your product is the solution to one of their problems. An easy-to-use solution increases customer satisfaction, reduces customer-support costs, and promotes repeat business.
- *Your company's image will improve* because a commitment to quality and customer satisfaction strengthens performance and reputation in the marketplace.

The primary goal of user manuals is to transmit information explicitly and accurately in order to help someone understand and use a product in order to get a job done.

A product is defined as a thing, a service, a procedure or process, an organization, a place, information, or an idea.

Fig. 3: Purpose of User Manuals

Manuals Are Part of the Product

A product is a tool, something that can satisfy a need or a want. A product can be a thing, a service, a procedure or process, an organization, a place, information, or an idea.

We live in the Information Age, a time when knowledge is fast becoming one of the most important products produced in the world economy. This means, for instance, that maintenance procedures, or an employee training program, or personnel information, or operating procedures can and should be considered *products*.

Further, the definition of user, customer, or audience can include in-house staff. In many companies, one division "sells" information, services, or hard goods to another. Progressive companies tend to view such activity as selling products to a market.

The *key feature* of a product is the *service* (benefit) it gives to your customers. This is what they will use to determine its value to them.

Think of it this way: Without a manual, a product is merely a *potential* product. When complemented by a good user manual, however, it becomes a *true* product, that is, a tool for solving your customers' problems.

2

HERE'S YOUR ROAD MAP

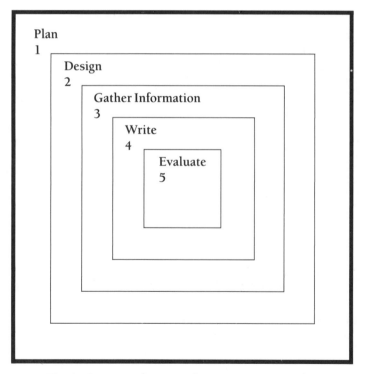

Fig. 4: Structured Approach to Writing, Example 1

1: Analyze	2: Design	3: Develop	4: Implement	5: Evaluate
(Plan)	(Design)	(Gather Information)	(Write)	(Evaluate)

Fig. 5: Structured Approach to Writing, Example 2

This chapter serves two purposes: First, it describes how the rest of this book is organized. In addition, it doubles as a road map to guide you through your own writing projects.

What is a road map? It is the big picture, the overall structure of a product. A road map gives a sense of perspective, allowing you to see and understand the general lay of the land before getting into the specifics.

A structured approach to manual writing helps you complete a project successfully. Figures 4 and 5 are different representations of the same structured approach to writing. Use the one you feel most comfortable with as your road map.

The first figure is a "nested" diagram, the second a "sequence" diagram. Both show that you must begin the writing process with planning and end with evaluation. However, this is not a strictly linear process—if the product specifications change during information gathering or writing, for example, you may have to loop back to the planning or design stages and make revisions. In fact, looping and revising may be necessary anywhere in the process.

What Do You Do at Each Stage of the Writing Process?

Plan (Analyze)

Define the project, objectives, audience, and project requirements. Identify top-level tasks.

Design (Design)

In the design stage you will:

- Define top-level conceptual design requirements
- Define manual specifications
- Establish page and text formats

Gather Information (Develop)

The information-gathering and design stages overlap, because "big picture" information and the outline belong to both stages.

In the information-gathering stage you will:

- Gather "big picture" information about the product
- Select a structural style
- Outline the manual
- Gather detailed product information, based on an approved outline

Write (Implement)

Use your outline and detailed product information to write the first draft of the manual. Follow the principles of good writing style.

Use your planning and design decisions to control the writing and to guide the manual through revisions and into production.

Evaluate (Evaluate)

Planning and design decisions give you a yardstick with which to measure how well your user manual meets project requirements. Monitor the manual for technical accuracy, usability, clarity, and consideration of your audience.

Publishing Cycle

- Plan
- Design
- Gather information
- Write/revise
- Format pages
- Handle artwork
- Evaluate (manual)

Production

- Text (hard copy, on paper)
- Video
- Online
- Audio
- Computer-based training
- Optical disk
- Diskettes
- Interactive videodisc
- Microfiche
- Hypertext
- CD ROM

Marketing Cycle

- Distribution
- Training
- Evaluation (sales &
  marketing)

Fig. 6: The Documentation Cycle

The Writing Process in Context

The writing process is part of the *documentation cycle,* which is composed of the publishing, production, and marketing cycles. This book deals primarily with the publishing cycle, as it applies to creating paper documentation, although we will also take a quick look at producing a document on paper.

3

PLANNING

Planning establishes the framework for writing a user manual and sets the stage for all subsequent tasks: design, gathering information, writing, and evaluation.

The decisions you make in the planning phase will be used during evaluation to measure whether the manual meets project requirements.

When you form a project team, its members may include the following, depending on the size of your company and how it is organized:

- Project manager
- Product expert(s)
- Subject-matter expert(s)
- Marketing personnel
- Sales personnel
- Legal counsel
- Graphic designers and artists
- Training and customer-support personnel
- Communications consultants

Since you are responsible for creating the manual, you should take the lead in asking the questions presented in this chapter and in the chapter on design. Your goal is to have the project team agree on the answers.

Quality Assurance/Quality Control (QA/QC): After your meetings with the project team, write a memo containing the planning questions and answers. Distribute copies of the memo to all members of the team. Any subsequent changes in planning decisions should also be written up and sent to all members.

- Why plan?
- What is the project? Define it.
- Who is the audience?
- What type of manual should we create?
- How will the manual be used?
- What is the product's expected life cycle?

Fig. 7: Planning Questions

At one of my seminars an attendee asked me, "What do I do when no one at my company wants to be on the project team? My boss wants me to handle everything by myself. And, in my case, I *am* the product expert. So what do I do?"

My reply was, "Ask *yourself* the questions in the chapters on planning and design. Make all decisions, and write them down. Then, before you go any further, send a memo containing the planning and design questions and your answers to your boss.

"Suggest meeting to go over the memo. If that is unacceptable, be sure you establish in writing a date by which you must be notified of any disagreements with the proposed project. After that date, send a brief memo stating that you will move to the information-gathering phase and handle the project as specified in the memo."

If you are in a similar situation, or if you are a small businessperson, an entrepreneur, or someone who works in an unstructured company, such an approach may work for you as well.

However, if you need help at any phase of the project, from planning through evaluation, and don't have an in-house project team, consider the following alternatives:

- Establish an advisory board of members of various backgrounds and areas of expertise.
- Hire consultants and other specialists as needed.
- Hire freelance writers and editors to work with you.

- Contact the Small Business Administration (SBA). They offer a range of services, including mentors.
- Ask colleagues from other companies for help.
- Barter for professional services with a businessperson who needs your skill and expertise in some area.
- Brainstorm by yourself or with others, using the techniques in this book.
- Join professional associations and business organizations. They usually offer a wide range of services.
- Get manuals from others in your business or industry and review them.

Why Plan?

A plan is an essential part of creating a good manual. Why?

- The product can change.
- The audience can change.
- Company operational procedures can change.
- Company personnel can change.
- Competition can force changes.

Without a plan, how will you know where you are in the project—and where you should be going? How can you track your work? How can you keep everyone on the project team coordinated and working together toward the same goal? Without a plan, you can't.

You must plan in order to be successful in the work environment *and* in creating a high-quality manual that meets project requirements.

Planning means *reconciling expectations*. Meet with key decision-makers—the project team—and hammer out an operating agreement regarding project requirements and expectations.

To do this, ask the *planning questions* that compose the rest of this chapter. You may want to add questions that specifically apply to your industry, company, or product. All decisions must be clearly defined, and understood and accepted by everyone on the team if the project is to be successful.

Don't let the manual get away from you!

Control the project from the outset!

What Is the Project? Define It.

Define the project to focus your attention and start the thinking process.

Ask for a project statement that answers these questions about the product:

- What is the name of the product?
- What does the product do? (What is its purpose?)
- Why would someone buy this product? (What problem does it solve?)
- How will the customer use the product?

Here are two simple examples:
Use the following technique to help define the project:

1. *List principal product characteristics:* features and usage.
2. *Ask for definitions* of terms you do not understand.
3. *Ask for additional information* if needed to continue discussing the product with the project team.
4. *Ask for more information about how the customer will use the product* if appropriate.

Example: The example project definition for software, given above, might prompt questions about these items:

- PC: Keyboard, monitor(s), computer, drives
- Disks: Definition of type, purpose, care, handling
- Start-Up: Cabling, powering up, problems
- Software: Definition, commands, options
- Hard Drive: Definition, features, organization
- System: Network type, error handling, messages

Who Is the Audience?

Why is this important? Because to create a usable manual, you *must know your audience.* Be sure that users can *learn* from your manual, that it *teaches* them how to use the product to get a job done. Too many manuals fail here, in that they function as little more than descriptions of the product.

Here are some questions to ask the project team:

1. Who is our audience? (See example groups below.)
2. What is the audience's skill level? What is their subject-matter knowledge?

Depending on the type of product you are writing about, "subject matter" can be defined as a field, a specialty, a business, or a topic. Here are some examples:

Field   Biology, Accounting
Specialty Molecular biology, Financial accounting

This is a new user manual for the **GreatWash** dishwasher, which cleans dishes, pots and pans, tableware, cutlery, and fine crystal.

The dishwasher will remove even the toughest stains and food particles, such as dried egg. Triple-spray action pumps hot water over dishes from several angles, while soiled water is continuously pumped out of the washing chamber. This key feature ensures that only fresh, clean water touches the items in the dishwasher. Food particles are ground in a special disposal system, stored during the wash cycle, then washed down the drain.

Although intended for home use, it has been built to industrial standards for many years of trouble-free service. This product offers five wash cycles, including water/energy saving cycles, and is one of the quietest models on the market. Racks may be adjusted to accommodate larger items. Special utensil, cutlery, and small-item baskets offer convenience and protection.

Whether the dishwasher is run once a week or three times a day, it ensures that all kitchen items used in cooking and eating are kept sparkling clean. This is part of good household hygiene.

Fig. 8: Example Project Definition for a Dishwasher

Business   Frozen foods, Banking
Topic   Staff orientation, Customer service

Subject matter can be a mix of these items. For example, customer service at a bank.

3. What background information might they need?
4. Given what we know about the project right now, which facts will help them use the product to get a job done?
5. Given what we know about the project right now, which

This will be an updated user manual for the installation of the FUN & GAMES 4.1 operating environment.

This environment allows users to take maximum advantage of the new 3-D video games in a full palette of colors. For multiuser games, like simulated 4-D Fractal Chess, multilevel, simultaneous windowing is available, allowing players to move into the game at different space/time coordinates and scaling factors.

The product offers real-time dynamic graphic display, full orchestral sound capabilities that interpret and play with shape and color using FFT calculations, and a color palette of 16 million shades for realistic action presentation. It runs all the newest, hottest, "you-are-there" video games. In addition, it allows users to play long distance since it comes with a 280.6 MBPS modem that is preset for the international OptoNet communications system.

The operating environment is intended to run on Earth-Q type machines that have at least one CD-ROM reader (or one old-style 10 MB floppy disk drive) and one 5 GB hard drive. The system must contain a minimum of 32 MB RAM. Control of installation may be handled through keyboard or voice recognition.

Fig. 9: Example Project Definition for Software

instructional techniques could we use in the manual to *teach* our audience and help them *learn?*

Audience Groups

To help answer these questions, think about your users. For example:

Experts in a field	Professional nonexperts
Technicians	Students
System operators	General users
Programmers	Children
Support staff	Internal (in-company) users

Audience Evaluation

For each group that is applicable, consider the following:

Attitude: What problem do the users need to solve? Why would they select our product for help?

Experience: How much experience do users have with our type of product?

Education: What is the audience's reading/comprehension level? How much should we assume, if anything? Does the product or subject matter dictate a range? What if we don't know? How can we estimate?

Now, write a brief profile of your audience.

What If You Have More Than One Audience?

If you have more than one audience, there are three basic ways to handle this situation:

1. *Write a separate manual for each audience.*
   This is usually done for audiences with widely differing needs or abilities.
   Example: General users and system operators. Both may use the same software, but from completely different perspectives.
2. *Group material for each audience into separate parts of a single manual.*
   This is usually done for audiences with needs or abilities that are

Introduction			Organization of This Manual
Audience Guide The contents of this manual are listed down the left side. A bullet (●) indicates which audience(s) should read each chapter and section.	System Adm. DP Mgr.	Data Entry	Sales Dept.
1.1 About This Manual	●	●	●
1.2 Product Overview	●	●	●
2.1 System Security	●		
2.2 Schedule Maintenance	●	●	
2.3 Department Maintenance	●		●
3.1 Sales Reports	●	●	●

Fig. 10: Audience Guide in Matrix Format

similar in some respects, yet different in others. The parts are completely separate, with no audience overlap. Each part might contain its own table of contents and index, for example.

Example: An updated product that will be used by novices and those who have experience with previous models/releases.

Example: One product used for many purposes or tasks. You might group material by task, thus, implicitly, by audience.

3. *Create an "audience guide" in matrix format,* showing which audience should read which chapter or section. The guide could be combined with the table of contents. Here there is audience overlap, because different audiences can read the same chapters, as shown in the figure above.

During one of my seminars on writing for users, I ended the discussion about audience by saying: "Remember, it's not enough just to build a better mousetrap. You have to . . ." and an attendee quickly interjected: ". . . *know your mouse!*"

- Instruction   operation-oriented: discusses procedures
- Theoretical   principle-oriented: presents the "why"
- Sales   selling-oriented: lists specifications, pricing, benefits
- Training   task-oriented: shows how to get a job done
- Reference   component-oriented: explains features/functions

Fig. 11: Types of User Manuals

What Type of Manual Should We Create?

Most products are accompanied by one or more of the types of manuals shown above. A single manual may consist of a mix of types.

Your initial decision about type may change as you discuss other planning and design questions.

A maintenance manual, for example, combines instruction and reference characteristics. It explains procedures necessary to keep the components, or parts, of a product in operating condition.

A manual for new employees in a customer-service department would probably combine elements of training and reference. First, it might explain the components, or parts, of the product (in this case, a customer-service program); then it would teach how to use the program to deliver good customer service. (Think of the new employees as the users, audience, or customers for this manual.)

How Will the Manual Be Used?

Consider how the manual will be used from two perspectives:

- Audience
- Total product package

- Instructor-led training
- Self-teaching
- Computer-based training
- At home
- At work
- As reference after training
- Repair/maintenance
- Other

Fig. 12: Manual Usage

Audience

As you discuss usage, you may find it necessary to redefine the type of manual that will best communicate what you want to say about the product to the audience. Decisions about usage will influence manual specifications, page and text formatting, structural style, and content.

Remember, no matter how well your users read and learn, you can make their job less difficult. You must know your audience and how they will use the manual in order to make reading and learning as easy as possible.

Total Product Package

In addition to deciding how the audience will use the manual, you must find out and/or decide how the manual fits into the total product package. You may find it necessary to redefine the type of manual, so that the entire package works together for your users. Ask these questions:

1. What accompanies the manual?
   Example: training videos, seminars, audio cassettes
2. Does the manual have to be entirely self-sufficient (no other materials accompany it)?

3. Are training courses or online tutorials included in the product package?
4. Does our company offer customer-support hotlines? Other types of support?
5. Does our company offer consulting or on-site service?

Your answers to these questions will influence the project team's final decisions about the type of manual and its design. The manual must fit into your *product communication system*.

What Is the Expected Product Life Cycle?

How long until the product is updated or replaced?

The answer to this question gives you a clue about the scope of the project, amount and type of artwork, and production issues and costs.

Example: A 140-page manual intended for a fairly small, specialized audience that is to be updated in nine to fourteen months will probably not require full-color illustrations, complex page formatting, and high-gloss paper. Nor would such a manual be printed on a printing press.

Instead, you might opt for black-and-white drawings, a simple page layout, and matte (nonglossy) paper stock. This manual would be reproduced on a copier.

Know the expected product life cycle in order to firm up your planning and make proper design decisions.

4

DESIGN

Design takes place within the planning framework; along with planning decisions, design decisions set the stage for gathering information, writing, and evaluation.

Quality Assurance/Quality Control (QA/QC): After your meetings with the project team, write a memo containing the design questions and answers. Distribute copies of the memo to all members of the team. Any subsequent changes in design decisions should also be written up and sent to all members.

If you do not have an in-house project team, consider the alternatives presented at the beginning of chapter 3.

- Design: Your top priority
- Manual specifications
- Page formatting
- Text formatting
- Project time estimates

Fig. 13: Design Issues

1. What are you looking for in this manual?
2. What do you feel is the most important part of this manual?
3. Describe four or five requirements for this manual. What type of response do you want users to have to it?
4. What percent of the manual is new? How much is a revision or update?
5. Who will be my product expert(s)? Subject-matter expert(s)?
6. Who will be my chief staff contact?
7. Is there any artwork (screens, diagrams, drawings, illustrations, photos)? Black-and-white? Color? Estimate how much of each type.
8. How will artwork be handled? Artist? Electronic files? Scanned images?
9. Shall I manage the project, or do you have a coordinator?
10. Are there company procedures for handling revisions?
11. Who has to review each draft/revision? Should marketing, sales, product development, internal auditing, legal counsel, or others be on the reviewer list?
12. Who has final approval of the manual?
13. What is the general time frame for the project? Any specific deadline?
14. Does the company have editorial style standards? If not, do we want to establish any for the manual?

Fig. 14: Top-Level Design Questions

Design: Your Top Priority

The above questions help reconcile expectations about the manual. Whether you work in-house or as a consultant to companies, reach an agreement with the project team on these issues.

Comments

Here is the reasoning behind the questions.

1–2. The first two questions ask the project team to identify the principal user benefit of the manual, and how the manual should show that.

Example: You could decide that you are looking for a manual that makes it easy for users to learn how to take advantage of your company's pickup and delivery services for media storage. In view of that, the most important part of the manual might be the step-by-step instructions on how to arrange such services, how to fill out the forms, and how to contact your firm if there are any service problems.

3. The four or five adjectives will give you a sense of anticipated emotional response. This is a very strong indicator of what members of the project team want to see when the manual is finished, so pay attention.

Example: Phrases such as "glossy," "lots of white space," "easy to read," "lots of diagrams," and "as few words as possible," are big hints about page and text formatting. They suggest small paragraphs, big margins, numbered steps, bulleted lists, typographic variations, and lots of visuals.

Example: A phrase such as "easy-to-find information" suggests a detailed table of contents, a list of figures, and a cross-referenced index. Also, perhaps, tabs, foldouts, appendices, quick-reference guides, charts, structure diagrams, or color-coded sections. Pages should have headers or footers.

Basically, you want clues about expectations regarding your manual's reading appeal and appearance *before* you begin work on it.

4. Whether the manual is to be new or an update is a factor in negotiating the general time frame or deadline for the project. If the time frame is short and nonnegotiable, you may need to pare the scope and content of the manual. Review planning decisions and discuss the answers to questions 1–3 above with the project team to determine what would be an acceptable manual, given the time frame.

A new manual usually requires *much* more work: interviews, hands-on learning about the project, more reviews, more artwork—everything. For an updated manual you *may* be able to use a lot of the material from the previous one, including some of the outline.

5. Get the names of product and subject-matter experts during design meetings. These folks should at the very least be informed by the project manager that they will be working with you on interviews, fact checking, and reviewing the manual for accuracy. Optimally, they would be present at meetings, since they are part of the project team.

6. The chief staff contact could be your boss, the project manager, or whoever is designated. This person may help schedule interviews with the experts, should be available to answer general questions during the project, and could function as a communications coordinator for the project team.

7–8. The quantity and type of artwork and how it is to be handled have a major impact on time and cost. Therefore, you must get a good estimate of what you will be dealing with, in order to judge whether it is too little or too much, given other planning/design decisions.

9. The project manager or coordinator handles the following: scheduling interviews, establishing the project schedule and keeping everyone on track, coordinating the flow of information within the project team, coordinating artwork, getting production bids, and scheduling production of copies of the manual.

10–11. Some companies have established procedures for handling revisions, others don't. Establish a procedure for the project, so that everyone understands what to expect. How many revisions? How much time allowed for each reviewer? Who reviews what? Do all reviewers review the same copy, or do reviewers each receive a copy for proofreading? What if someone falls behind schedule? Reviews can be—and often are—a major bottleneck in staying on project schedule. Do *not* underestimate the time it takes a reviewer to check facts or procedures for accuracy. Build a realistic schedule with the project team.

Establish a list of reviewers. Everyone on the list should agree to be on it. Given what you know at this point, explain the project schedule, what each reviewer is expected to do, and approximately how much time reviewers will spend on the project at each phase. Later, as you move into the revision stage of the project, you will fine-tune these plans.

12. Whoever has final approval should be at all planning and design meetings. If this isn't possible, and/or that person will not be able to review

the manual until it is ready to go into production, find out what has to be done to ensure that the manual will indeed receive final approval, without problems.

13. Given what you know about the project so far, is the deadline realistic? If not, what can you trim (in scope or content) from the manual and still create a good document? Can you negotiate a realistic deadline, given what the project team or manager would like to do?

Not allowing enough time to produce good work is often a problem. Part of the solution lies in having the project team, including managers, agree on planning and design issues. Professional communicators, or those with some experience in what it takes to get the job done well, should lead the way in establishing scheduling guidelines.

Remember that the manual is an integral part of the product. Whether your company creates software, financial services, electric generators, cars, training programs, dishwashers, or health services, remember that those products were not planned, designed, and built overnight, or with little time, effort, or cost. A good manual won't be either.

14. Does your company have an in-house style guide for written communications? If not, you may need to develop an editorial style guide in order to ensure consistency. Some common trouble spots are: page and text formatting, terms and names, abbreviations, capitalization, punctuation, units and measures, acronyms, and spelling.

Example: Don't say *13 inches* in one part of the manual, *13 in.* in another, and *13″* in still another. Choose one, and be sure that you stick to it.

Manual Specifications

The questions in the following figure help reconcile expectations about the usability, appearance, and production of the manual. Whether you work in-house or as a consultant to companies, reach an agreement with the project team on these issues.

1. How many manuals are to be written?

2. What is the title of each manual?

3. What is the estimated number of product features, parts, processes, commands, screens, menus, options, or pages in each manual?

4. How many copies of each manual are to be produced?

5. Will there be a table of contents, list of figures, list of tables, or index?

6. What will the final page size be?

7. How "camera-ready" should the pages be delivered?

8. Does the company have guidelines for page and text formatting? Who is to handle page and text formatting?

9. What type of paper stock (weight, type, and color) and ink color(s) will be used for the cover, if any? Any artwork on the cover?

10. What type of paper stock (weight, type, and color) and ink color(s) will be used for inside pages?

11. How is each manual to be bound? (*Example:* spiral binding, ring binder, perfect binding, saddle stitching)

12. How is each manual to be produced? (*Example:* copier, small press, full-color web press)

13. Before final work on the manual, will it be alpha- or beta-site tested?

Fig. 15: Manual Specifications

Comments

Here is the reasoning behind the questions.

1. Given the planning and design questions that you and the project team have discussed so far, you may have decided that more than one type of manual is required.

2. Each manual must have a "tentative," or "working" title during the project. This helps team members keep track of which project they are working on. As soon as possible, decide on the "real," publishable title, so

that the manual's text doesn't have to be continually revised to reflect name changes.

3. Product experts should be able to help you estimate the size of the manual by supplying this information. You may want to discuss the deadline again.

4. The production house (copy shop, printer, etc.) will need to know how many copies are to be produced in order to schedule your job. Marketing and sales staff, among others on the project team, should be able to guide you.

5. Any manual over 20 pages should have a *table of contents*. Any manual over 50 pages should have an *index*. If your manual contains more than 5 figures or tables, it should contain a *list of figures* or a *list of tables*. These "pointers" or "links" help users find information. They cut down search time and help users learn about your product and use it to get a job done. Remember, manuals are not read cover to cover, like novels.

Many word-processing and desktop-publishing programs allow you to mark text electronically and then generate a table of contents, lists, and an index. You will still have to format them, however, to make them consistent in typeface, spacing, and layout.

Other "pointers" that make a good manual great:

- Tabs

  Index tabs are often shaped like a half-moon, with the flat edge flush with the outside edge of the page. Many dictionaries use this type of tab.

  Diecut tabs are cut into regular or irregular shapes from paper. Such tabs are usually attached to their own tab sheet and precede a chapter or section.

  Bleed tabs are printed on the page and continue off the page (bleed) when the edge has been trimmed away. They are sometimes called *reverse out tabs,* because the word, letter, or number on the tab appears in white surrounded by a solid block of color.

  Color-coded first pages can serve as a type of tab and are used to indicate the first page of a chapter or section.

- Tear-out job aids

  Cards or pages that show key information, relationships, or facts required to do a job. For example, a company organization chart in a training manual for new staff members.

- Quick-reference cards
  Cards that list the principal commands or steps needed to do a job, with little or no explanation. They are meant to be used after reading the manual.

- Foldouts for large diagrams or spatial representations

- Color-coded sections

These are *not* necessary; to justify including them in the total product package, be sure they help users find information, or guide them through a task. They must be as thoughtfully planned and designed as the rest of the manual, and must complement it.

6. Page size helps create the manual's—and your company's—image. Generally, in-house manuals and those destined for specialized, "niche" audiences measure 8.5″ × 11″ (American standard size) or 210 × 297 mm (European A4 standard size, which equals 8.27″ × 11.69″). Manuals published for the mass-market often measure 6″ × 8.5″ (American) or 182 × 257 mm (European B5, which equals 7.36″ × 10.40″).

7–8. *Camera-ready* means that the page is ready to go to production: all page and text formatting has been done and approved, and all artwork inserted electronically or manually (this is called *paste-up*).

Find out whether your company has a preset format you should use, and verify with the project team that it is appropriate for your manual. If no guidelines exist, bring in a few sample pages from manuals similar to the one you have to create.

If your responsibilities include planning, design, and writing copy (text), but *not* page and text formatting, you will probably deliver *manuscript pages* to your art department or a freelance artist. When you think of manuscript pages, think of your typical college term paper—that's generally what they look like. Ask the artist or graphic designer how to format (on disk or paper) your manuscript pages in order to make the artist's job as quick and easy as possible. You may also want to work with the artist to select typefaces and formatting styles for the camera-ready pages.

As computers and desktop-publishing programs have become more common, more and more writers are being asked to handle page and text formatting.

9–10. Have you been to a copy shop or printer lately to check out paper stocks and how they are used? Have you met with a production specialist to learn about inks and paper types, weights, and colors, and look at sample jobs? No? Well, make an appointment! You need to see and feel the stuff in order to make good choices for your manual. While you're there, you can also make contacts for production bids. You should visit at least three firms: one that handles small jobs, another for medium-size jobs, and a third for large, complex jobs. Pricing varies dramatically, based on number of original pages, number of copies, whether there is any color or photos, type of paper, binding, and so on.

Keep in mind that very pale green, blue, or ecru paper may be easier on the eyes than white in some work environments. A high-gloss white will glare under many types of lighting. Even a matte (non glossy) white reflects much more light than other colors.

11. Who is your audience? How will the manual be used? How long until the product and manual will be updated? Do you need to be able to replace some, but not all, pages periodically? Do you need to ensure that pages cannot be easily removed from the manual? Consider these and other planning/design decisions to select a binding.

Spiral binding is also called "GBC" binding. The spiral is usually made of plastic or metal. This binding is commonly used on manuals that are less than 1.5″ thick. This binding lies flat when the manual is open, so the text is easy to read.

Ring binders are widely used in the computer/software industry. Pages have three holes punched in them (two in Europe) and are inserted into the binder. This type of binder allows for easy replacement of pages for frequent updating. Other advantages are that it lies flat when open for easy reading and it stands upright on the shelf. An easel-type ring binder allows users to work on a task and read the manual at the same time.

Perfect binding is typical of hardbound or paperbound trade books. Pages are stitched and glued, or just glued into the spine of the book. Most books in a bookstore are perfect-bound. Like the ring binder, books stand upright on the shelf.

Saddle stitching is generally used on booklets, pamphlets, and manuals that contain up to 50 pages. The spine of the booklet is stapled, usually near the top and the bottom, then folded.

12. How many original pages are there? How many copies of the manual are to be produced? Is the artwork all black-and-white figures, screens, and diagrams, or are there photos and color? How long until the manual will be updated? Answers to these questions will help you determine the best value for your production dollar.

Here's a quick rule of thumb for determining cost-effectiveness, given only black-and-white figures:

Copier: Fewer than 2,000 copies
Small press: Between 2,000 and 10,000 copies
Large press: More than 10,000 copies

13. *Final work* means electronically marking and generating the "pointers" (table of contents, lists, and the index). *Alpha-site* testing takes place in your own company. *Beta-site* testing happens when you send the product to another company, or a focus group, for testing.

Testing without the pointers does mean that the testers will have to read from cover to cover, checking content and verifying that they can really follow procedures to get a job done. If material needs to be added, deleted, or moved, however, you won't have to re-generate and re-format the pointers. This saves money and time.

On the other hand, your company may want testing to include the pointers, to be sure they really help users find information. The benefit here is that testing is closer to real-world situations, and some of the most important parts of the manual are tested and judged. The expense of re-marking and re-generating the pointers may prove to be a modest investment that creates a superior manual for your market.

Page Formatting

Page formatting is also called "page layout" or "page design." Bad page formatting tends to push the reader away from the page, making it difficult to concentrate. By contrast, good page formatting invites the reader to use the manual and makes learning easier.

Whenever you find a manual that contains appealing, well-formatted

Page size
Headers
Footers
Page numbers
Quantity/style of art
Placement of art on page
Placement of text on page
White space
Justification
Line spacing
Margins
Typeface(s)
Print quality

Fig. 16: Elements of Page Formatting

pages, copy a page or two and save them in a "page format file." Then, when you meet with the project team, you can present samples of possible page formats for your manual. This will speed the decision-making process.

The total graphic image of the page includes the above elements.

Figure 17 shows an example of bad page formatting.

Text formatting is also a problem in this example. See the next section, *Text Formatting*, for more information.

Figures 18–20 show examples of good page formatting.

-2.17-

This example shows bad page format. Notice that it violates just about every rule of good page formatting. Among the problems are no headers or footers, little white space, small margins, no variation of typeface, text that looks more like a binary stream than something meant for human eyes, and page numbers that resemble section numbers. Could you imagine having to read 300 pages of this to learn how to use a product?

This manual also contains very few figures, and they are crudely drawn. Given that the product is based on a new, complex technology, and that users must learn to understand the technology as well as use the product, many more figures should have been included in the manual.

The table of contents lists only chapter titles, even though some chapters contain up to three levels of section numbering. There is no list of figures, and no index! Clearly, whoever wrote this manual does not understand that users must be able to find information quickly and easily. A manual is not a novel or a magazine.

2.4   This Section Title is Too Far Down on the Page

In addition to bad page format, text format is also bad. There are no numbered lists or steps, no columns, no text boxes or tables, and no graphic lines to separate text. The basic text style is "narrative," that is, paragraphs. While narrative is very useful in manuals, 300 pages of it reduces the manual's "usability index" to almost zero.

Fig. 17: Example Bad Page Format

Chapter Title

The chapter title states the overall subject of a chapter. Everything in the chapter must belong to the "subject group." The first paragraph in a chapter presents the subject in greater detail, including purpose and any pre-requisites for reading or using material in the chapter. It may also describe benefits or results derived from using the material.

Let's pretend that this chapter discusses the physical (not procedural) features of a company's on-the-job safety program. The features are hierarchically ordered, from the plant (building) down to each workstation. The names of the features will become section titles.

Plant

This paragraph describes the general construction features of the plant. Specifics include tolerances for natural disasters and environmental controls. All facts and figures are supported by test results.

First Feature.   The principal feature affecting plant safety is given here. It might be site-specific, such as geographic location or soil type.

Second Feature.   The second most important feature is given here. It might be construction-specific, such as 12-inch thick, steel-reinforced walls.

Third Feature.   The third most important feature is given here.

Security System

This paragraph describes those parts of the security system that apply to worker safety. If this manual were to be distributed to employees, for example, more sensitive levels of the system might not be included.

Alarm System.   This feature might discuss the company's UL-certified alarm system that constantly monitors certain locations.

Fig. 18: Example Page Format for a Reference Manual

Manual Title - Chapter Number   **Page Number**

● File Menu ●

1. Save   - Save a file to a disk.
2. Retrieve   - Get a previously saved file.
3. Copy   - Copy one file to another file.
4. Rename   - Give a file a new name.
5. Delete   - Erase a file from a disk.

6. HELP   - Get HELP for this menu.
7. EXIT   - Go back to the Main Menu.

Type the number of the option, then press <Enter>.

In this training manual example, there are more screens than text. Each screen shows one step in solving a problem. Here, we are going to learn how to save a letter.

Accompanying text tells users what to type into the program, which keys to press, and which results to look for.

Notice that paragraphs are very short. This helps users move quickly through the text.

At this point in the lesson, we have already learned how to create a letter.

To save the letter you have created, type [1] or [S], and then press <**Enter**>.

You will see this message.

After your file has been saved, the program returns you to the **File Menu**.

Now saving file ...
Please wait.

Product Name   Program version number and release date

Fig. 19: Example Page Format for a Training Manual

Chapter # - Page #　　　　　　**Manual Title**
　　　　　　　　　　　　　　　Chapter Title

Copy

3.3 COPY

This paragraph explains when to use the **Copy** option, and why. List any "default" conditions first. If users must select another option or do something else *before* selecting **Copy**, mention it in this paragraph. If there are any restrictions on using **Copy**, mention them in this paragraph.

Any general or specific results should be mentioned here.

How to select Copy:

1.　　Open the **File** Menu.

2.　　Type [3]

　　　or

　　　[C] to select *Copy*.

3.　　Press <**Enter**>.

4.　　Type in the letter of the drive and the new file name.
　　　Example: [**F:\newname**]

5.　　Press <**Enter**>.

This copies the file. You may insert a pathname in front of the file name. If the subdirectory is new, the program will automatically create it. See section *Directories and Pathnames*, in this chapter, for more information.

A *Copy* message appears in the lower-left of the screen. The message will display the drive, pathname, and file name.

Company Name　　　　　　　　　　　　　　　　　　Product Name/Release Date

**Fig. 20:　Example Page Format for a User Manual
That Combines Reference / Training**

Indents
Tabs
Font point size
Font weight (bold, italic)
Graphic lines
Running glossary (margin
    keywords)
Paragraphs
Text boxes
Tables
Bulleted lists
Numbered sections
Numbered lists
Numbered steps
Highlighted text blocks
Character sets (icons, math)
Columns

Fig. 21: Graphic Techniques for Text Formatting

Text Formatting

Like bad *page* formatting, bad *text* formatting tends to put the reader off, while good text formatting makes reading and learning easier.

The visual cues listed in figure 21 will make your text more inviting, effective, and encouraging to users.

Look again at the sample pages from the page formatting section. Notice that *text* formats change, depending on the type of manual and material. Three of the most popular text formats for user manuals are:

Narrative   Moves from the general to the specific.
                Changes focus from one subject to another.
                Presents and develops a concept.
                Describes a product or a process.
                Prepares the user for instructions or procedures.

This chapter presents the FILE MENU and its options. Use this menu to manage text and graphic data associated with the manual on which you are working.

The FILE MENU is shown below. We will discuss how to save, copy, delete, and rename files.

Enter the FILE MENU by selecting option FILE in the MAIN MENU.

Fig. 22: Example Narrative Text Formatting

Cookbook	Gives a clear sequence of chronological steps (instructions).
	Shows users how to get a job done.
Action/Result	States the action the user is to perform and gives the result.
	Contains little or no detail or description.
	Appears often in user manuals for highly interactive products.
	Presents a summary of commands.

To install the program, follow these steps:

1. Insert Disk 1 into Drive A.

2. Type [**CD/**], then press <**Enter**> to move to the Root Directory (Main Directory) on the hard disk.

3. Type [**a:install**], then press <**Enter**> to run the installation program.

The installation program is menu-driven, so you can install all or only part of the program.

Fig. 23: Example Cookbook Text Formatting

Moving around the Text Editor

PRESS KEY	RESULT
$<ALT\rightarrow>$	Move right one field
$<ALT\leftarrow>$	Move left one field
$<\uparrow>$	Move up one field
$<\downarrow>$	Move down one field
$<\rightarrow>$	More right one character
$<\leftarrow>$	Move left one character

Fig. 24: Example Action/Result Text Formatting

Project Time Estimates

How do you estimate the time needed for writing a user manual? First, you must answer most of the planning and design questions. Other factors vary from project to project and person to person. Only you can know the answers, but these are the principal issues to consider:

Project Issues

- How much do you know about the product and subject matter?
- Who is your audience?
- How complex is the manual, in terms of product, training needs, artwork, formatting, examples, and level of detail?
- How much production time is required to produce a finished, marketable manual?
- How much artwork is there, who is creating it, and how will it be merged into the text?
- How many reviewers are there, how fast and thorough are they, where are they located, and what are your review procedures?

Personal Issues

- How familiar are you with the word-processing or desktop-publishing package(s) you will use to produce the manual?
- Is producing the manual your sole responsibility, or are you expected to add it to other duties?
- How fast do you work?
- What is your approach to the project? Structured? Or random, thoughtless, and disorganized?

Rule of Thumb

I have asked a number of professional, freelance writers for time estimates, *per page,* for user manuals. The estimates range from 1 to 1.5 hours per manual page, including information gathering, an outline, a first draft, two medium-size revisions, proofreading, and printing camera-ready original pages. This assumes that most artwork is created by an artist or graphic designer (not the writer) and then integrated with the text on a computer.

Sound too fast? Then double the time for your own project estimate. The less experience you have, the more time you should allow. It is better to finish the project well within your time and cost budgets than to over-run either. A little padding can come in handy if there's an emergency or unexpected delay.

With experience you will improve your project estimates.

5

INFORMATION GATHERING
AND THE OUTLINE

This chapter gives you pointers for gathering information about the product and creating an outline. You will learn to:

- Gather "big picture" information about the product
- Conduct information-gathering interviews with product experts
- Understand the purpose and use of an outline
- Select a structural style for your outline
- Gather detailed information about the product

Your goal in this stage of the manual-writing process is to acquire and understand information about the product, particularly its operations and applications.

- First, get the "big picture"
- Next, create an outline
- Last, get the details

Fig. 25: Information and Outline Issues

```
PARTS of the product
NAME of each part
FUNCTION(S) of each part
RELATION of one part to another
_____

PARTS may be features or components,
operations, applications, tasks, or commands
```

Fig. 26: "Big Picture" Information

First, Get the "Big Picture"

The "big picture" is a road map of the product. It shows the product's features, components, operations, applications, tasks, or commands.

The figure above shows the "big picture" information you must get in order to create an outline for the manual.

Key Information Resources

Before or during your first information-gathering interview, ask for the following resources. They will help you learn about the product and prepare for your interviews, and may reduce interview time.

While all of these resources may not be available, your product development, marketing, or operations departments should have some of them.

1. **Hands-on tour**
   Schedule this at the top of your list. See the product, and go over its operations. Go through a sample application, if possible.
2. **Structure diagrams**
   These show the parts and their name. Diagrams also reveal how the parts fit together.

3. **Fact sheets**
   These generally list the function of each (major) part.
4. **Help, error, or glossary messages**
   These tip you off about potential problems for users.
5. **Older versions of the manual**
   If you are writing an update, you may be able to use much of this material, including the outline.
6. **Operating descriptions**
   These give information on operating the product, but are not necessarily task-oriented. You may also find information on the function of parts of the product.
7. **Flowcharts**
   These generally show workflow. They would be helpful for a manual geared to training, processes, or tasks.
8. **Marketing literature**
   This describes key features and/or operations and user benefits.
9. **Product specifications**
   These list important product or usage information, and operating requirements.
10. **Application examples**
    These will tell you how the marketing and product development people view the product, and what they feel its major benefits are to users, that is, what principal problems the product is designed to solve.

What If the Field or Product Is New to You?

If the field is new to you (new subject matter), you will need a fast learning curve. Here are some methods for acquiring subject-matter knowledge:

- Ask an expert to recommend journals, textbooks, or summaries.
- Ask an expert to recommend videos or training courses.
- Conduct subject-matter interviews with experts, focusing on how their information applies to the manual you have to create.
- Plan to have subject-matter experts available to answer questions *as needed* throughout the project.
- Plan on working extra smart and extra hard.

If the *product* is new to you, use the planning, design, and information-gathering techniques presented in this book to learn about the product and create the manual. If you don't have in-house product or subject-matter experts, consider the alternatives presented at the beginning of chapter 3.

Interviewing the Experts

Experts tend to be nice people. They are a diverse bunch and, like everyone else, they are busy. Most of all, however, product or subject-matter experts *are your most important resource for information about the product.* Depending on the manual, they may include sales reps, computer programmers, customer service people, marketing executives, and others.

Back in the planning stage, you and the project team established a list of experts who agreed to be interviewed, right? You probably also decided who would be interviewed for which parts of the manual: who will talk with you about features and operations, who specializes in training and applications, and who can give you hints and tips based on customer feedback.

Make Appointments

When you call to make appointments, remind your interviewees of the following:

- You will probably need to ask them questions throughout the project, with the bulk of the interviews and questions at the beginning.
- You are interested in learning about the product from the user's perspective: "How do I use it to get a job done?"
- They will have a chance to review your work, since they are on the list of reviewers. (They will "fact check," not proof copy or style.)
- You will need to be notified about changes in the product if you are creating the manual during product development. (Establish a notification procedure, then be sure to take the initiative in checking for changes.)

Prepare for Interviews

Never walk into an interview unprepared. It is unprofessional and unproductive. Prepare yourself by learning as much about the field and product as you can ahead of time, using key information resources and other suggestions in this chapter. Make lists of questions for the product or subject-matter expert. Use Post-it notes or paper clips to mark pages in key resource materials or other documents where you have questions.

In order to get the most out of each interview, prepare an *interview outline*. If you plan it well enough, you can use it now to gather "big picture" information, and later to gather details.

The principal benefits of an interview outline are these:

- You gather information in a consistent order. This makes the information easier to use in outlining the manual and in writing the first draft.
- You could distribute copies of the interview outline to product and subject-matter experts and have them fill in "big picture" information. Then, schedule interviews to clarify any problems.
- You make it easier for the product and subject-matter experts to work with you, because you ask for information in consistent order.
- You can use the same interview outline later to gather details. The initial "big picture" information will serve as a reminder or prompt.
- You establish an "audit trail" to help verify and track your work. This serves as another Quality Assurance/Quality Control (QA/QC) check.

The interview outline allows you to set specific goals for each interview, which focuses everyone's attention on working toward the same result. It systematically breaks the product down into manageable parts. This approach curbs the tendency toward tangential discussions during interviews, and ensures that you end up with valid, useful information that is coherently organized.

Do Not Make Assumptions

As you prepare for your information-gathering interviews with product and subject-matter experts, beware of making assumptions!

Do not assume that you and the experts understand and define in the

BIG PICTURE
Name of part:
    (diagrams/schematics will show parts)
Function of part:
    (purpose—what does it do?)
Relation to other parts:
    (prerequisites for using part)
    (result of using part)

DETAILS
Selection/access procedure(s):
Part/operational details:
Usage procedure(s):
Usage problems/tips:

PARTS may be features or components,
operations, applications, tasks, commands

Fig. 27: Example Interview Outline for a Reference Manual

same way the product, its operations, procedures, terms, or applications. Ask for explicit definitions and explanations. *Asking questions is your job!*

If you do not understand the answer to a question, ask again. Try rephrasing the question. Ask for an analogy; what is it *like* or *similar to*. If the information is not clear to you, then it will not be clear to your customers.

Interview the Product and Subject-Matter Experts

Arrive a little early at the appointment.
Bring copies of the interview outline you have developed.
Bring relevant key information resources, with questions marked.
Bring note pads and pens.
Use a tape recorder, if allowed and appropriate. Remember to bring extra tapes. A tape recorder will free you from trying to write down every

1. What are the product's most important features?
2. What are the product's limitations?
3. What is the product's competition? How does it rank?
4. Why would someone choose this product over other methods of solving a problem or getting a job done?
5. What are the key benefits to the user of each part?
6. Is the product used the same way every time to get a job done? Or, are there many methods of ordering tasks and procedures?

Fig. 28: Additional "Big Picture" Questions

word and asking the interviewee to repeat material. It will allow you to concentrate on listening, asking questions, and learning.

Use the interview outline to keep the interview on track. Explain to the expert why you have prepared it and what the benefits to both of you will be.

Go over the material to be covered in the interview until you understand it. Do not accept technobabble. If the expert really understands the product and subject matter, you will eventually elicit a clear explanation. Remind the expert of who the audience is, and the type of manual you are creating.

Completing the "Big Picture"

Above are some additional "big picture" questions that may help you outline the manual.

Next, Create an Outline

The outline of the manual creates a bridge between the planning/design stages and the gathering of detailed information. It reflects all the thinking and work you have done so far in defining product purpose, audience,

1. Use the planning and design information in this book to define all project requirements.

2. Gather "big picture" information about the product.

3. Select a structural style for the outline/manual that allows you to satisfy project requirements.

4. Write the outline down on paper.

5. Get the outline approved.

6. Use the outline to gather detailed information about the product.

7. Use the outline to write the first draft and all revisions. It serves as a Quality Assurance/Quality Control (QA/QC) check.

Fig. 29: General Method of Creating and Using an Outline for a Manual

type of manual, document usage, "big picture" information, and other project requirements.

Trying to write a manual without an outline is an exercise in grief and agony. Why is the outline so important?

- Writing requires you to process and integrate an incredible amount of information, data, and project requirements. Complexity increases exponentially in proportion to the length of the document. Without an outline, you don't know where you are going, and any mistakes will snowball until you have a total mess.

- Manuals are often thought of as "linear" or "serial," because they are on paper—one page after the next. In fact, however, a manual is really more like a web: A change in one part usually affects the rest of the manual. An outline provides large-scale control.

- A bald, brutal fact of writing is that structure is fundamental to understanding, learning, and usability. It is fundamental to keeping a reader's interest and attention. If you do not have a solid, thought-out outline, *nothing* will save your manual. The outline is the document's power generator.

- You have to think through the problem of writing a manual fairly

As you write your outline, here are some questions to guide your effort:

1. Are you using a structural style? Which one?

2. Is the structural style appropriate, given:
   product purpose
   audience
   type of manual
   how the manual will be used
   "big picture" information
   other project requirements

3. Do your main headings tell the story, from beginning to end? Can you scan the headings and get an accurate sense of the "big picture"?

4. Do minor headings properly subdivide the main topics?

5. Is your "big picture" information correct?

6. Is the scope of content appropriate for your audience and the type of manual?

Fig. 30: Questions to Guide Writing an Outline

thoroughly to create an outline. You now know what you must do and how to go about doing it. You have a road map. You are in control.

What Is Structural Style?

Structural style is the *order* in which you organize the information in your manual. In this section, we will discuss types of order and how you select one to be the structural style of your manual.

The product for which you are to write a manual has *already* been physically or logically designed as a "whole" that contains "elements," a "system" that contains "parts," or a "general" process that contains "specific" elements:

SYSTEM   General category to which something belongs.
          Examples:
          Venn diagram showing entire task-system
          System diagram of a software application
          Structure diagram showing entire product
          Flowchart of entire process
          Company organizational chart

SET   Major subdivisions of the system.
          Examples:
          Tasks that make up a system
          Menus within an application
          Modules that make up a product
          Groups of procedures or operations in a process
          Departments in a company

PART   The elements in each set.
          Examples:
          Steps that make up a task
          Options that make up a menu
          Parts that make up a module
          Procedures or operations within a group
          Sections within a department

"Big picture" information shows you how the product developers have designed the product. What you must do is select a structural style that preserves this design while transmitting it to users in a clear and usable way.

User manual outlines are usually organized by one of the structural styles shown below. You should already be familiar with some or all of these styles, since they represent fundamental, universal ways of ordering information. If you have studied languages, literary analysis, linguistics, mathematical and algorithmic logic, or computer science, you will have been formally introduced to these and other orders. Those who studied journalism will recognize "who, what, when, where, why, and how," although not in that sequence.

Spatial Order	Used to explain the parts of a product: features and functions. Organized by physical or logical location.
Chronological Order	Used to show sequence or order of occurrence of instructions, steps, processes, development, or evolution. Organized by occurrence in a timeline.
Cause/Effect Order	Used to show which agent/problem (cause) produces which results (effect); or vice versa. Organized by cause-effect or effect-cause (general to specific, or specific to general).
Hierarchical Order	Used to rank quantifiable criteria, such as size, cost, alphanumeric value, frequency of operation, durability of goods, importance, authority/responsibility, or ease/difficulty of performing tasks. Organized by ascending or descending order.
Similarity/Difference Order	Used to show similarities or differences of products, processes, tasks, developments, phenomena, organisms, symptoms, data, and other information that can be compared. Organized by similarity/difference, or other point of comparison.

Fig. 31: **Structural Styles for User Manuals**

The outline *is* the structural style of the manual. Its purpose is to show large-scale or "big picture" structure. The outline will eventually become the table of contents.

As a rule of thumb, *spatial order* works best for reference manuals, while *chronological order* is a good choice for training and procedure manuals.

Now let's take a closer look at each structural style.

Structural style is used at all levels of the manual: in the outline (large-scale), in the paragraph (mid-scale), and in the sentence (small-scale). In any given manual, you will probably need several styles.

Examples of Spatial Order:

Logical organization of software applications
Physical organization of computing devices
Location of workstations in a production facility
Layout of a factory floor (physical space)
Work flow on a factory floor (logical space)
Assembly of a diesel engine
Appearance of a shoe
Specification of dimensions of a dishwasher
Location of continents and countries

May Be Graphically Represented By:

Structure diagram (logical or physical)
Floor plan (location or layout)
Work flow diagram
Exploded-view diagram
Drawing
Blueprint
Map

Fig. 32: Spatial Order

Example: Organize the outline in chronological order to indicate a series of lessons or tasks that must be sequentially learned. Within each lesson, select chronological order for steps or directions. Where appropriate, use cause/effect order to help users solve problems and correct their errors. At the end of each lesson or task (chapter) use hierarchical order to summarize, in order of descending importance, what the user should have learned in the lesson. If the manual will be used in a classroom, you might use similarity/difference order to create an ideal timeline against which actual progress could be plotted.

Note: See the section on *Mid- and Small-Scale Structural Style* in chapter 6 for more information on structural style applied to paragraphs and sentences.

Examples of Chronological Order:
Sequence of steps in getting a task done
Stages of a manufacturing process
Production schedule for a user manual
Development of a product
Changes in pollution levels on Earth
History of a company

May Be Graphically Represented By:
Numbered list
Flowchart
Calendar
Timeline
Line graph
Date chart

Fig. 33: Chronological Order

Chapter Template

Here are some tips for organizing a chapter or section. Use this template to get yourself started, but remember that every manual is different.

Chapter templates are generally organized by order of descending importance (hierarchical order). Why? Because readers of a user manual want to know the most important information first. This means that you must proceed from the general to the specific—from the system ("big picture") to the parts (details).

Sample template:
BIG PICTURE INFORMATION
- chapter or section title
- purpose of the chapter/section and its content
- user benefit—why would user read chapter/section or use content?
- prerequisite(s) for reading chapter/section or using content
- result(s) of reading chapter/section or using content

Examples of Cause/Effect Order:

Impact of environmental pollutants on lung diseases

Impact of various manufacturing methods on
product quality

Diagnosis of product malfunction by listing potential
causes

Identification of repair procedures to correct a
problem

May Be Graphically Represented By:

Bar graph

Bar graph, grouped columns, or paired pages

Cause/multiple-effect tree or diagram

Cause/effect table

Fig. 34: Cause/Effect Order

- list of subtopics in chapter/section (if applicable)
- statement of objectives at beginning ("what you will learn"—if applicable)
- summary at end of chapter/section ("what you have learned"—if applicable)

DETAILS
- selection/access procedures
- part/operational details
- usage procedures
- usage problems/tips
- warnings or notes

Within the "details" section of the template, you will use mid- and small-scale structural styles to present information in the proper order. See chapter 6 for more information.

Examples of Hierarchical Order:

Frequency of problems during operation
Sizes of files in a database
Sequencing tasks by descending order of importance
Alphabetized entries in a dictionary
Objectives ranked by descending priority
Cost of products ranked in ascending order
Lessons organized by order of increasing difficulty

May Be Graphically Represented By:

Bar graph
Line graph or percent table
Sequence or nested diagram
Sorted list in ascending order
Numbered list
Bar or line graph
Table or numbered list

Fig. 35: Hierarchical Order

Sample Outline

The purpose of this example is to show you an outline that solves a simple design problem. You may want to use it as a general model for your own work.

Planning Decisions Context

The product is a new software application called WREN (Wonderful Room ENgineering), which is used to analyze structures for soundproofing. It is the only product on the market that focuses on this aspect of building design.

The product is intended for engineers, acousticians, and structural specialists who have a background in structural and acoustic engineering.

The user manual outlined in this example is a reference manual. It must

---

Examples of Similarity/Difference Order:

Comparison of a new process for getting a job done to
an older, error-free process

Organizing a manual for multiple audiences

Showing correct/incorrect methods of operating a
product in a training manual

Comparison of data on products according to cost,
features, and markets

May Be Graphically Represented By:

Paired bar graphs or pages

Matrix (table)

Multiple columns or paired pages

Table or histogram

Fig. 36: Similarity/Difference Order

be primarily self-teaching, although the company will offer training seminars and a customer-service hotline. (The reference manual is also accompanied by a training manual.)

Design Decisions and "Big Picture" Information Context

We need to show lots of screens and figures to make the product as easy to understand and use as possible. This is especially important since it is new to the market. Users must be able to find information quickly, so we must include a table of contents, a list of figures, and an index. The manual will include a wall chart showing a structure (organizational) diagram of the entire application. Page size is 8.5″ × 11″. Reference material will be printed on pale blue paper. Everything else will be printed on white paper. Black ink will be used on all inside pages. Inside pages will be three-hole drilled and inserted into the company's ring binders.

We will use page and text formatting similar to those presented in examples in this book. Special emphasis will be placed on formatting text in a "graphic" way, because studies show that users respond better and learn more quickly when they see short paragraphs and sentences, bulleted or numbered lists, numbered text boxes with titles, big margins, and lots of white space.

WREN is menu-driven, with a relational database that allows all screens in the program to share the same data. This ease of use is a key feature, because the application is complex.

The program was well designed. It is very interactive, displays prompts for every required response or data-entry field, and provides helpful error messages. The analysts and programmers worked with a focus user group to develop a product that is easy to use *from the customer's point of view*.

There are five menus in the program. After engineers enter modeling information, they may display the results on screen, or print them out on a plotter.

The Outline

The manual is outlined by spatial order, since a menu-driven system is organized by logical location. Also, a reference manual explains the features and functions of the product, which must be presented by logical-location order. (The accompanying training manual will link the features and functions together in chronological order to show how to use the product to get a job done.)

Title Page
    Copyright notice
    Title of manual
    Name of product and release/version number
    Date of release
    Company name, address, phone, fax
    Note: When the manual is packaged (in clear shrink-wrapping) for inventory and shipping, the title page lets everyone see at a glance what is in the package.

Table of Contents

List(s) of Figures/Tables

Preface (or "Introduction" or "Getting Started" or "Read Me First")
    Purpose of Product and Manual
    Audience
    How is the Manual Organized?
    How to Use the Manual
    Other Resources
        accompanying manuals (e.g., training)
        training seminars available
        customer-service hotline
        online tutorials

List of Enhancements (if the product is an update)

1. Overview
   1.1   What is WREN?
   1.2   Why is WREN Different from Other Structural Design Programs?
   1.3   What are WREN's Principal Capabilities?
   1.4   How will WREN Help You Design Better Soundproofed Buildings?

2. Manual and Operating Conventions
   2.1   Notation Used in This Manual
   2.2   Screen Layout
   2.3   Special Function Keys
   2.4   Graphic Pre-Processors
   2.5   How to Get HELP
   2.6   How to EXIT WREN

3. WREN Organization
   3.1   Product Structure
          Show structure diagram
          Discuss top-level function of each menu
          State prerequisites for using menus
   3.2   Database
          Define modules, sets, and elements

Define permissible data types
Discuss hard-disk organization

4. WREN Filenames
    4.1   Principal Files
          Sizes, usage, restrictions
          File types, by extension and function

5. Main Menu
        Show Main Menu screen
        Briefly explain each submenu, using "big picture" information:
    5.1   File Menu
    5.2   Acoustic Data Menu
    5.3   Structural Data Menu
    5.4   Scaling Menu
    5.5   Output Menu

6. File Menu
        Show screen
        Give purpose, any prerequisites before using, results
        Tell users how to access the menu
    6.1   Create File (first option on File Menu)
              Give purpose, any prerequisites before using, results
              Tell users how to access option
              Discuss operational details
              Explain usage procedures
              Give tips for using option, handling problems
    6.2   Copy File (second option on File Menu)
              Give purpose, any prerequisites before using, results
              Tell users how to access option
              Discuss operational details
              Explain usage procedures
              Give tips for using option, handling problems
    6.3   Delete File (third option on File Menu)
              Give purpose, any prerequisites before using, results
              Tell users how to access option
              Discuss operational details

Explain usage procedures
Give tips for using option, handling problems
. . . *and so on for each option*

7. Acoustic . . . 10. Output
For a real project, you would continue the outline in detail, as shown above for chapter 6, File Menu. Keep chapter organization parallel for ease of use; a chapter template will help you do this.

11. Appendix
    11.1 User Tips
    11.2 Error Messages

12. Glossary

13. Bibliography

14. Index

Sample Outline

This example shows you an outline for a manual that describes services.

Planning Decisions Context

The product is environmental management services, including consulting, evaluation, and problem-solving.

It is offered to public and private clients, many of whom know very little about environmental management.

The user manual outlined in this example is a sales/marketing manual. It must highlight the company's reliability, expertise, and professionalism. The sales staff will use the manual as a primary sales tool, frequently sending it to prospective clients before the first sales call. Therefore, it must make a terrific first impression.

Design Decisions and "Big Picture" Information Context

The manual needs only an organizational chart; no other visuals are necessary. A short table of contents will list only the titles of each chapter.

There will be no list of figures or index. Chapters are not to be numbered. Diecut tab sheets will precede each chapter. Page size is 8.5″ × 11″. The inside pages of the manual will be printed in black ink on high-quality gray bond paper. The cover and tab sheets will be printed on card stock in full color, using reverse print (white print on a darker background). It will be spiral bound.

Graphic designers will handle page and text formatting. We suggest that they consider selecting a sleek typeface, and use columns, bulleted lists, and graphic lines in formatting.

The company offers services in these areas: site investigations, analytical services, environmental audits, evaluation of alternatives for waste reduction, treatment and disposal, site remediation, and permitting assistance.

We need to validate the company in the eyes of prospects by showing that they can place their trust and confidence in its staff and track record.

The Outline

The manual is outlined by hierarchical order, in order of descending scope and importance of subject.

Table of Contents

Company Purpose and Mission

Client Services
    Site Investigations
        description
        site characterization
        site investigation plan
        evaluation
    Analytical Services
    Environmental Audits
        reasons for audits
        approach to audits
        evaluation
        response to results
    Evaluation of Alternatives for Waste Reduction, Treatment, and
        Disposal

methods
implementation of results
Site Remediation
  review of site data
  scope of analysis
  feasibility study
  evaluation of alternatives
  safety and QA/QC plans
  schedule
Permitting Assistance

Quality Assurance
  Guidelines
  Testing
  Methods and Procedures
  Projects

Professional Staff
  Organizational Chart
  Credentials
  Resumes

Experience
  This chapter contains 30 synopses showing the company's qualifications for solving a broad range of complex environmental problems.

Facilities
  Laboratories
  Mobile Response Centers
  Waste Transportation
  Stabilization Facilities
  Hazardous Waste Disposal Facilities
  Waste Treatment Facilities

Equipment
  Laboratory Equipment   (listed in alphabetical order)
  Response and Remediation

Last, Get the Details

At this stage of the project, you and the project team have made planning and design decisions, you have interviewed product and subject-matter experts to gather "big picture" information, and your outline has been written and approved.

Now you must gather and organize detailed information about the product so that you can proceed to writing your first draft of the user manual.

What Information Do You Need?

First, review the outline and your "big picture" information resources and interviews. Given this information, you should have a clear idea of which details you must get.

The next step is to schedule "details" interviews. Use techniques similar to those you used in gathering "big picture" information, just change your focus. It's time to zoom in on each part of the product for a close-up. Before your first interview, review the "details" section of your interview outline.

Finally, meet with your product experts. As you gather details, *follow your outline for the manual* and use the "details" section of the interview outline. Remember that you must explain the product *from the user's point of view*. Put yourself in your customer's shoes and ask: "What do I need to know in order to understand this product and use it to get a job done?"

And keep in mind decisions made about the following:

- product purpose
- audience
- type of manual
- how the manual will be used
- project requirements

The example shown in figure 37 assumes a single-user system. What other details might you need for the following computer products?

- Network
- Modem or other communication device
- Server

Operating conventions (e.g., use of <Enter> key)
Units of measurement
Special commands: definition, function, result
Function keys: definition, function, result
Types of files and purpose of each
Database organization
Moving around screen and screen layout
Definition of all terms
Each menu/option: purpose, selection, usage, problems
Each data-entry screen: purpose, access, usage, problems
Each data-entry field: purpose, access, usage, problems
Maximum character input in each field
Data types and restrictions in each field
Required vs. optional input fields; results
Default for each field
Security and any access restrictions

Fig. 37: Example Software Application Details for a Reference Manual

- Printer or other output device
- Peripherals

How Do You Organize the Details?

The manual exists on two levels:

Intellectual Level = Thinking = Planning, Design, Outline
Physical Level = Files = Storage Media

As you gather details, all that paper has to go somewhere, in some order. Since you are gathering details according to your outline, ask yourself this question: "Given the structural style I have selected for the outline of the manual, what is the best method of organizing my files?"

- Meet with your product and subject-matter experts
- Test the product yourself
- Check your information resources (notes, files)
- Review example applications of the product
- Go to a library to search for additional information
- Call a government agency (for information or a publication)
- Dial a database

Fig. 38: How to Clarify Problems

Examples:

- by features
- by tasks
- by procedures in an operation
- by commands
- by functions
- by problems/errors

Label each file, using the outline of the manual as a guide.

If you really want to be good to yourself, *within each file folder* organize information according to your chapter template.

Now that you have transformed the intellectual level into the physical level, you can concentrate on your work instead of trying to remember where all the information is located. When it is time to write the first draft, all of this thinking and organizing will pay off.

How Do You Clarify Problems?

As you gather details (and probably while you are writing the first draft and making revisions), the product will undoubtedly change, if it is currently under development. This is a fact of life in most companies. Product modification is so constant at most software firms that the industry has a name for the phenomenon: vaporware.

Important!

1. Date your questions!
2. Date the answer and note the source!
3. Be sure that all changes are properly filed!

Fig. 39: Keep an Audit Trail When You Clarify Problems

Other problems that may occur:

- What if you find an error as you work with the product?
- What if something strikes you as illogical, but you're not sure?
- What if you don't understand a procedure, operation, or process?
- What if you thought you understood all terms and definitions, but now you're baffled by one or more?
- What if you need more background information about the use of the product by the intended audience, or about the subject matter?

When you get answers to your questions, *keep an audit trail of all changes!* An *audit trail* is not only useful for writing the first draft, editing your work, and controlling the project, but it serves as proof of your work in case you need to verify what you have done on the project.

6

PRINCIPLES
OF GOOD WRITING

Now that you have planned and designed your manual, created an outline and gotten it approved, and gathered all the details, you know *what* you want to say. As you prepare to write the first draft, you must also consider *how* you are going to say it.

Your writing style is unique, because it comes from your nature, experiences, personality, abilities, and thinking. Good style also depends on understanding the principles of good writing.

The principles of good business and technical writing will help you communicate. Learn them well and practice them daily, and you will improve your writing style.

- What is good writing style?
- Mid- and small-scale structural style
- What about spelling, punctuation, and grammar?
- How do you handle numbers, equations, units, and symbols?
- What about abbreviation and capitalization?
- List of language references

Fig. 40: Writing Style Issues

What Is Good Writing Style?

Remember that the primary goal of user manuals is to transmit information explicitly and accurately in order to help someone understand and use a product in order to get a job done.

A good writing style helps you achieve that goal. Strive to develop a style that can be described by the following adjectives:

Accurate

Make the content of the manual as true and accurate as possible. This means that you must know your subject matter and have gathered correct information. Errors cost time, money, and customer goodwill.

Further, you have a moral obligation to give your readers factual information. Accuracy is the least they can expect from your work. Without accuracy, the rest is useless.

Consistent

Refer to a part, process, fact, procedure, idea, thing, service, organization, or operation in the same way *every time you write about it*. Yes! Use the same word or phrase! Over and over and over! Again and again! Do *not* vary your references to something by using synonyms or different phrases or terms. Why?

Manuals are not leisure reading or entertainment, so referring to something in even two different ways is likely to confuse and irritate your readers. New terminology implies a new idea, new information, or a new fact.

Long ago in composition and creative writing classes you were urged to find fifty ways to express an idea or to refer to something. Such variations are wonderful and necessary in fiction, poetry, and many other types of writing. Do this in a manual, however, and you pull the rug out from under your readers' feet, because they will be forced to pause and ask: "Is this something new, or is it merely a new way of referring to it?" When they finally figure out that you are simply referring to one thing in many different ways, they will not thank you for it. You will have cost them time and confusion by impeding their learning.

Watch especially for consistency in:
- Page format
- Text format
- Terms and names
- Definitions
- Abbreviation
- Capitalization
- Punctuation
- Units and measures

Fig. 41: Consistency in Writing Style

Clear

Your objective is to make the content of the manual immediately understandable and usable.

The greater your ability and knowledge in all four areas, the clearer your writing will be. If someone tells you that your work is not clear, use these questions to analyze where the problem might be, then take steps to correct it.

A list of language references is given later in this chapter. You might also consider purchasing software programs such as *Grammatik* and *Right-Writer*. These programs analyze business and technical writing and suggest improvements in grammar, syntax, use of adjectives, length of sentences, use of subordinate clauses, and so on. If you feel you need more work in the craft of language, and want a teacher to critique your writing, check out classes offered for adults at universities and community colleges.

Some final thoughts on "clear":

- Be careful of getting too "cute" or "clever" in your writing. It tends to irritate most readers and makes learning more difficult.
- Be careful of telling stories or going off on a tangent. If an anecdote does not serve the purpose of your manual, based on your planning and design decisions and your outline, get rid of it.

Problems of clarity fall into one or more of these categories:	To analyze the problem, ask these questions:
PLANNING	Do you understand the purpose of the product and the manual? Do you know who your audience is? Do you know how the manual will be used?
DESIGN	Did you answer the top-level design questions? Did you establish page and text formatting guides? Do you have an outline based on planning and design decisions?
INFORMATION	Do you know *what* you want to say? Do you understand the material? Do you have the right material, based on your outline?
LANGUAGE	Do you have a reasonable understanding and grasp of the "craft" of language—spelling, grammar, syntax, punctuation, vocabulary, and word usage?

Fig. 42: Clarity in Writing Style

- Be careful of humor. Generally, avoid it in manuals. What is funny to you may be extremely insulting to a reader.

Short and Simple

As a rule of thumb, keep your paragraphs, sentences, and words short and simple. This means:

- one subject to a paragraph
- 6–8 lines in a paragraph
- 25 or fewer words in a sentence
- small words

When writing a manual, choose the smaller word. For example:

Smaller Word	Larger Word
food	comestibles
house	domicile
drink	beverage
watery	aqueous
guess	conjecture
start	commencement
shorten	abbreviate
copy	duplicate
cut	incision
end	terminate
name	nomenclature
next	subsequent
tiny	minuscule

Fig. 43: Simplicity in Writing Style

Most people learn best when material is presented in "chunks," with the subject clearly defined. The eye can grab and digest 6–8 lines quickly. Sentences longer than 25 words are more complex and tend to be less easily understood. The key is to vary sentence length, for interest and readability, while keeping most sentences fairly short.

What is a "small word"? Plain language. Generally, a "small word" has only one or two syllables and is of Anglo-Saxon, as opposed to Latin, origin.

Keep it short and simple and your writing will be clearer and more concise. Do not build monuments to obfuscatory sesquipedalian tergiversation.

When writing a manual, be concise. For example:

Wordy	Concise
at this point in time	now
until such time as	until
prior to that time	before
hold a meeting	meet
on a weekly basis	weekly
has been widely acknowledged to be	is; seems; appears
exhibits the ability	can
on an annual basis	yearly
with reference to	about
in some cases . . . in other cases	sometimes
the reason why is that	because; due to
on the occasion of	when
is equipped with	has; contains
it is clear that	clearly
a large number of	many

Fig. 44: Wordy vs. Concise in Writing Style

Concise

Concise means "not wordy." When writing is wordy, suspect one of the following:

- The writer has not planned or designed the manual, does not have an outline, and does not really know what to say.
- The writer does not understand the subject matter.
- The writer is trying to hide something from you.
- The writer has developed bad language habits and is not thinking.

Thus, the writer beats around the bush. When you write, get to the point. Go for substance, not filler.

Figure 44 shows examples of wordy vs. concise language. Notice that the concise phrase does *not* alter meaning.

Redundancy, saying the same thing twice, is another form of wordiness. One of the words in the phrase is "extra" and must be deleted.

In these examples, the underlined word is redundant and should be deleted.

continue <u>on</u>
<u>absolutely</u> perfect
<u>completely</u> unique
any <u>and all</u>
<u>advance</u> plan
<u>current</u> status
<u>first</u> introduction
<u>basic</u> essentials
joined <u>together</u>
<u>true</u> facts
<u>past</u> history
repeat <u>again</u>

Fig. 45: Redundancy in Writing Style

Active

Prefer active voice to passive voice. Why? Active voice shows who is responsible for the action. It adds conviction and liveliness to your writing, and is more concise than passive voice. Readers find "action verbs" appealing, because such verbs are direct and show motion.

Imperative

Use direct commands when giving instructions. Readers understand commands more easily and quickly than indirect requests.

Specific and Concrete

Use facts, figures, and data in your writing. Avoid vague, general terms. When you claim that your product performs a certain function, provides some type of benefit, or meets industry standards, you must supply the facts that prove your statement.

Active Voice

She <u>poured</u> the chemical.
He <u>breathes</u> the air.
The dog <u>will eat</u> the food.

Passive Voice

The chemical <u>was poured by</u> her.
The air <u>is being breathed by</u> him.
The food <u>will be eaten by</u> the dog.

Fig. 46: Active vs. Passive Voice in Writing Style

As you read the example in figure 48, imagine that you want to buy a new heating system. Which of the two paragraphs gives you more useful information for comparison shopping or making a decision?

Notice that the specific and concrete paragraph names the system immediately, so the reader starts to create a mental image, a "hook" on which

Imperative

<u>Move</u> the cursor to the first field.
<u>Enter</u> data in this form.
<u>Rotate</u> the dial once.
<u>Press</u> the F1 key.

Indirect request

You should move the cursor to the first field.
This form needs to have data entered into it.
You will probably find it helpful to rotate the dial once.
The F1 key should be pressed by the operator at this time.

Fig. 47: Imperative vs. Indirect Request in Writing Style

Vague and General

In most cases we feel it is useful to keep in mind that you can save a small fortune in heating costs by carefully regulating the controls on your new system. It is efficient, reliable, and cost-effective.

Specific and Concrete

Your new HotAir Heating System can save you up to $4.00 each day—a 40% reduction in the average monthly heating bill in your area. How? Just keep the temperature range set between 68°F–72°F. In test after test, this UL-certified system has proven to be 99.9% repair-free during its 25-year operating life.

Fig. 48: Vague vs. Specific in Writing Style

to hang new information. While the vague paragraph *claims* you can "save a small fortune," the specific paragraph *shows* you, by stating dollar amounts and savings percentages. Specifics such as "68°F–72°F," "UL-certified," "99.9% repair-free" and "25-year operating life" give the reader facts, figures, and data that make the product seem appealing.

Present

Use the present tense whenever possible. When readers use your manual, their time frame is the here and now, not the past or future. The past tense is useful mainly for describing actions that are genuinely completed at the time of writing, such as experiments or research. For more information on tense, and verb conjugation in general, see the list of language references at the end of this chapter.

> **Parallel**
>
> They studied <u>history</u>, <u>mathematics</u>, and <u>chemistry</u>.
> They learned <u>to play</u> tennis, <u>to swim</u>, and <u>to ride</u> a horse.
>
> **Nonparallel**
>
> They studied <u>about the past</u>, <u>mathematics</u>, and <u>how matter
> is constituted</u>.
> They learned <u>to play</u> tennis, <u>swimming</u>, and <u>the art of
> horseback riding</u>.

Fig. 49: Parallel vs. Nonparallel in Writing Style

Parallel

When two or more ideas are similar in nature, express them using the same part of speech (pair nouns with nouns, infinitives with infinitives, and so on). Parallel construction is clearer, more concise, and easier to understand.

Notice that the predicate (stuff after the verb "studied") in the first parallel sentence in figure 49 contains a list of nouns: history, mathematics, chemistry. The second contains a list of infinitives: to play, to swim, to ride.

By contrast, the predicate in the first nonparallel sentence contains a prepositional phrase ("about the past"), a noun ("mathematics"), and an adverbial phrase ("how matter is constituted"). The second contains an infinitive ("to play"), a gerund ("swimming"), and a noun phrase ("the art of horseback riding").

Although nonparallel constructions are grammatically correct, they are stylistically less elegant. Readers absorb information more easily in parallel form.

Watch especially for parallel construction in numbered or bulleted lists.

Informal

Use a conversational tone when writing a user manual. "Tone" is the attitude you wish to convey about the subject to the reader. When writing a manual, your goal is explanation and teaching. Show your readers respect, and make them feel welcome.

Some tips:

- Address your readers as "you" from time to time.
- Use pronouns such as "we" and "they" occasionally.
- Use the present tense (action-oriented).
- Read your writing aloud. Are your sentences varied in length? Does your writing sound fairly conversational? Would you use the same words if you were speaking to someone?

Objective

Focus on the content, not your opinion of it. Remember, a manual must help users understand your product and learn to use it to get a job done. Substantiate your claims with facts, figures, data, and results.

Interesting

Develop your "story" and keep readers moving through the manual. How?

Some tips:

- Follow your outline.
- Use the principles of good writing style presented in this chapter.
- Use *comparisons* to communicate new or difficult-to-grasp ideas or products.
- Use *images* (words that create pictures in the mind).

Many new products are based on complex technologies where parts, features, components, processes, or operations are beyond the range of human perception. Think of fields such as computer science, molecular biology, electronics, or cosmology. They involve microcircuits, millions of instructions processed in a second, atoms and molecules that require

Example 1

Description:
Red blood cells are biconcave and flexible. Their purpose is cellular oxygenation.

Image:
Red blood cells look like a crimson-velvet frisbee with a dent in the middle of both sides. Supple and elastic, they squeeze through the tiniest blood vessels to carry the breath of life, oxygen, to each cell in your body and remove carbon-dioxide waste.

Example 2

Description:
The read-write head of a hard disk rides about seven microns above the surface of the platter.

Image:
Each strand of hair on your head is about 75 microns wide. Compare this to the seven-micron distance between the read-write head and the platter of a hard disk.

Fig. 50: Description vs. Image in Writing Style

electron scanning to be seen, complex electron trajectories, even the infinity of space. We are asked to understand and use things beyond the range of our own ears, eyes, or hands.

Therefore, you must connect what cannot be heard, seen, or touched to what can. Use images that show relation to the human scale of perception.

Mid- and Small-Scale Structural Style

Mid-scale (paragraph) and small-scale (sentence) structural styles are similar in type and purpose to large-scale (outline) structural styles, which we previously discussed in *What Is Structural Style?* in chapter 5.

Their purpose is to show relationships among topics, or parts of a topic, in order to help users understand your product and use it to get a job done.

We will consider three issues:

- Paragraph order
- Paragraph unity
- Subject sentence

Paragraph Order

How you order paragraphs depends on where you are in your outline and chapter template.

For example, let's suppose that you are writing a training manual for new employees and have selected a hierarchical order for your outline, in which information is organized by order of descending importance. You also developed a chapter template so that all chapters would be organized as consistently as possible.

Now what?

Pick a chapter and review the chapter template. It shows the order of information in that chapter. Next, select a section and ask yourself: "What am I trying to say here?" For example, are you trying to describe an object, teach someone a security procedure, discuss an aspect of corporate operations, or alert new employees to rules, regulations, and disciplinary measures?

Description of an object seems to call for spatial order of paragraphs; teaching someone procedures might require chronological order; corporate operations might also require chronological order, or perhaps hierarchical order; while a discussion of rules, regulations, and disciplinary measures might be organized by cause/effect order.

What you must do is select a mid-scale structural style that helps you develop each section in every chapter. Styles can vary from section to section. It all depends on what you are trying to explain.

Depending on the mid-scale structural style you select, use words similar to the examples shown above, so that your paragraphs "flow" in the proper order:

Spatial order shows *where* something is physically or logically located.
Chronological order shows *when* something happens.
Cause/Effect order shows *who* does *what* (agent that causes result).

ORDER				
Spatial	Chronological	Cause/Effect	Hierarchical	Similarity/ Difference
above	during	therefore	most	like
below	before	if ... then	highest	similar to
horizontal	finally	since	lowest	analogous to
vertical	previous	caused by	fewer	comparable to
behind	later	because	greater	unlike
next to	while	due to	larger	in contrast
internally	after	based on	smaller	correlative
externally	first	as a result	decreasing	also
adjacent to	next	consequently	more	on the other
diagonally	last	produced by	less than	hand
overhead	earlier	so	degree of	not only ...
around	in turn	accordingly	least	but also
... etc.	... etc.	... etc.	... etc.	... etc.

Fig. 51: Mid-Scale Structural Style

Hierarchical order shows *why*, based on quantifiable criteria that can be ranked.
Similarity/Difference order shows *how* things are alike or different, based on one or more points of comparison.

Paragraph Unity

Focus your readers' attention by putting *one and only one subject in each paragraph*. You must state the subject of the paragraph in the first sentence (the *subject sentence*). Every other sentence in the paragraph must support and develop the idea you presented in the first sentence.

ORDER	Example subject sentences. Underlined words indicate order of paragraph.
SPATIAL	The File Menu is one level <u>below</u> the Main Menu. The switches are located <u>in front of</u> the rotor.
CHRONOLOGICAL	<u>Before</u> installing the kitchen sink, turn off the water. <u>Next</u>, assemble the flyrod.
CAUSE/EFFECT	<u>If</u> you have properly installed the operating system, <u>then</u> you will see these messages:
HIERARCHICAL	The following parts are listed by <u>decreasing</u> cost.
SIMILARITY/ DIFFERENCE	Computers can now analyze measurable <u>differences between</u> these noise-annoyance frequencies.

Fig. 52: Small-Scale Structural Style

Subject Sentence

The subject sentence is the first sentence in a paragraph. It announces to the reader what the idea or subject is, and indicates how the paragraph is organized.

Hints on Analyzing Paragraphs

Ask yourself these questions to analyze your work and take steps to improve it:

- What is the key idea (subject sentence) in each paragraph?
- If there is more than one subject, then how many paragraphs are needed to ensure that each paragraph contains only *one* subject?
- Within each paragraph, is the *subject sentence* first?
- Are paragraphs ordered according to a mid-scale structural style, so that they develop the material?

What About Spelling, Punctuation, and Grammar?

They are part of the craft of language, the toolkit that we use for writing. No one can ever know too much about language and using it well. You will always have questions about craft, whether you are reading or writing, and should own at least a couple of reference books. Refer to the list of language references in this chapter.

Software programs such as *Grammatik* and *RightWriter* are designed to analyze business and technical writing from the perspective of craft. You may find them very helpful, in addition to the thesauruses and spelling checkers that accompany most word-processing programs.

The rules of thumb for writing a user manual are these:

- Use rules of standard English.
- Strive for flawless spelling, punctuation, and grammar. These are the most basic elements of the craft of language, and you should be able to use them fluently.

Clarity and elegance in writing flow from planning, design, information, style, and craft. If your manual needs more attention to craft, use the following figure to help analyze your work and locate the problem.

How Do You Handle Numbers, Equations, Units, and Symbols?

When you use numbers, equations, units, and symbols in a manual, *the rule of thumb is to be consistent.*

Numbers

Use the list in figure 54 to avoid the most common problems.

Equations

Pay special attention to equations when editing and working with proofreaders, typesetters, graphic designers, or painters. Most people find equations to be a particularly difficult notation system. To avoid common problems:

Spelling	
Grammar	(parts of speech)
Punctuation	
Syntax	(order of words; creates meaning)
Vocabulary	
Phonetics	(pronunciation/sound production)
Semantics	(usage and meaning of words)

Fig. 53: Craft of Language

- Watch placement of superscripts and subscripts.
  Examples: H_2O vs. HO_2
  $$x^2 \text{ vs. } x_2$$
- Center equations on the line.
- Keep all same-level operators on the same text line.
  Examples of operators to watch for:
  $$+ \qquad *$$
  $$- \qquad =$$
  $$/ \qquad (\ ) \text{ or } [\ ] \text{ or } \{ \ \}$$
- Set equations off in the text. Don't crowd. Leave plenty of white space around each equation.

Many software programs now offer "equation palettes," which allow you to create equations within the document. This can save typesetting costs and reduce errors.

Units

Look for tables of units of measure in general and field-specific dictionaries, if the product and subject-matter experts cannot supply you with what you need. If you use units of measure in the manual, be sure to include a table in a glossary or appendix.

Use the list in figure 55 to avoid the most common problems.

1. Write out numbers below 10, when used as adjectives, *unless* in a series:

   two nails   (*not* 2 nails)
   five clocks   (*not* 5 clocks)
   BUT: 35 hammers, 2 nails, and 14 flanges

2. Write decimals and fractions as numerals, not words:

   0.75   3.1415   ½   ²⁄₇   ⅓

3. Write units of measure, page numbers, percentages, money, and ratios as numerals, not words:

   10 feet   page 7   56 percent
   $4.50   2:1

4. Use commas to separate millions and thousands:

   1,350,000   4,675

5. Spell out millions, billions, and other large numbers:

   1.5 million   *instead of*   1,500,000
   67 billion   *instead of*   67,000,000,000

6. Use scientific notation where appropriate: 240×10^6

7. Hyphenate a number and a unit of measure when they form a compound adjective:

   6-week-old chick   11-pound baby

8. If two numbers modify a noun, write one as a word:

   eleven 10-inch nails

9. Do not begin a sentence with a numeral. Use a word: Write "Ten" not "10" to begin a sentence.

Fig. 54: **Numbers**

1. Write units as *accepted* words or symbols. Do not make them up. Check dictionaries or field-specific references.
   Examples:

Unit	Symbol
second	s
kilogram	kg
radian	rad

2. Fractions are not plural. No amount that is one or less can be plural.
   Examples:

   0.75 *cup* of flour   (less than one)
   1.50 *cups* of flour   (greater than one)
   ⅐ *ton* of coal   (less than one)
   0.66 *pound* of meat   (less than one)

3. Place secondary units in parentheses after the primary unit. Maintain this order throughout the manual.
   Example:
   10-meter (32.8-foot) length of pipe

Fig. 55: Units

Symbols

Symbols can make your text clearer, easier to read, and more concise. Here are rules of thumb for using symbols:

- You may not invent symbols for a product or field. There are general, standardized tables for fields such as chemistry, engineering, mathematics, computing, medicine, and so on. Many companies have established style guides that contain symbols they use. Find out what they are.
- Less *is* more; use too few symbols rather than too many. Remember, your audience must decode symbols. Too many get in the way.
- Define the symbols you use the first time they occur. Also, include a definition table in a glossary or appendix.
- Each symbol must represent *one and only one* idea, term, unit of mea-

sure, variable, element, operation, part, and so on. If you work in one division or department of a company, check to verify that other divisions or departments do not use the same symbol to mean something different.

- Since symbols substitute for words, they must fit into the grammatical structure of the sentence. To test, write out the symbol in full. Are your articles, pronouns, and verbs still correct?

What About Abbreviation and Capitalization?

Abbreviation

The rule of thumb is to avoid abbreviation as much as possible. Like symbols, abbreviations must be decoded by readers. Too many abbreviations get in the readers' way. If an abbreviation is not immediately clear to you and the reviewers, then spell out the word in full. This is especially important when you are writing for a general, nonexpert audience.

As with symbols, standardized tables of abbreviations exist for many fields and businesses. Many companies create in-house style guides containing their own abbreviations. Do *not* arbitrarily abbreviate words. Do the following:

- Check with your project manager or a communications department head to see if your company has an in-house style guide.
- Head for the language-reference section at a good bookstore.
- Check out the reference section at a library.
- Work with the project team to establish agreed-upon abbreviations. Get them approved by the project manager, then send everyone a copy of the list. Be sure that the abbreviations you use in the manual are defined the first time they occur, and that you include a definition table.

Capitalization

The rules of thumb are these:

- The first word of a sentence is always capitalized.
- The first letter of a proper noun is always capitalized.

The Chicago Manual of Style is an excellent reference for rules of abbreviation. The following guidelines will help you avoid the most common problems:

1. Be consistent! Abbreviate a word the same way every time you use it.

2. Define the abbreviation the first time it occurs. Include a definition table in the manual.

3. Never abbreviate someone's name, unless you are given permission to do so.

4. You may abbreviate titles and armed-forces rank designations before or after a name, as specified by the possessor of the title or rank. If a name is not used, then you must spell out the title or rank.

5. Abbreviate private and government agency names only as specified by the agency.

6. Abbreviations are customarily used in footnotes and in bibliographies.

Fig. 56: Abbreviation Guidelines

List of Language References

Here is a list of references that you may want to have in your library. There are many others on the market, but these will get you started and provide answers to many questions.

Barzun, Jacques. *Simple and Direct.* New York, NY: HarperCollins, rev. ed. 1984.

Bernstein, Theodore. *The Careful Writer.* New York, NY: Atheneum, 1965.

Corbeil, Jean-Claude. *The Facts on File Visual Dictionary.* New York, NY: Facts on File Publications, 1986.

Flesch, Rudolf. *The Art of Readable Writing.* New York, NY: Collier Books, rev. ed. 1984.

Follett, Wilson. *Modern American Usage: A Guide.* New York, NY: Hill and Wang, 1966.

Fowler, H. W. *The Dictionary of Modern English Usage*. Belfast, ME: Bern Porter, 1985.

Greenia, Mark W. *Consultant's Guide to Computer Abbreviations and Acronyms*. Sacramento, CA: Lexikon Services, 1988.

Hopper, Vincent F., and Craig, R. P. *1001 Pitfalls in English Grammar*. Woodbury, NY: Barron's Educational Series, Inc., 1986.

Hopper, Vincent F., Gale, Cedric, and Foot, Ronald C. *Essentials of English*. Woodbury, NY: Barron's Educational Series, Inc., 3rd ed. 1982.

Strunk, William, Jr., and White, E. B. *The Elements of Style*. New York, NY: Macmillan, 1979.

The Chicago Manual of Style. Chicago, IL: The University of Chicago Press, 13th ed. 1982.

Roget's International Thesaurus. New York, NY: HarperCollins, 1984.

Webster's Ninth New Collegiate Dictionary. Springfield, MA: Merriam-Webster, Inc., 1989.

Technical dictionaries for your field.

Reference texts for your field.

Capitalize the first letter of a proper noun:

1.	Academic-degree abbreviations:	R.N., Ph.D., D.Sc.
2.	Astronomical bodies:	Earth, Venus, Milky Way
3.	Books, magazines, plays, newspapers:	*Newsweek, The New York Times*
4.	Brand and trade names:	Tide, Corningware
5.	Clubs and associations:	The United Way
6.	Companies and institutions:	International Business Machines
7.	Geographic names:	Europe, Africa, Antarctic
8.	Holidays:	Independence Day, Memorial Day
9.	Days and months:	Wednesday, November
10.	Nations, nationalities, languages:	Peru, British, French
11.	Proper names:	Barbara Walker, Tom Baker
12.	Direct quotations (first letter):	He said, "Let's walk up the hill."
13.	Salutations and complimentary closes:	Dear Mr. Dawson, Sincerely
14.	Streets, highways, buildings:	Main Street, Sears Tower
15.	Titles:	Justice O'Connor, Chancellor Weiss

Fig. 57: Capitalization Guidelines

7

THE FIRST DRAFT

The first draft represents the culmination of work you have done so far on the manual: planning, design, and information gathering. As you begin to put your ideas and information down on paper, follow your outline and use the principles of good writing.

What Is the Most Efficient Way to Do a First Draft?

The nonwriting aspects of a first draft affect the outcome of the manual. They set the stage for the revision process, determining whether it will be more or less difficult to manage.

Organize the first draft in this way:

- *Use your planning and design decisions.*
  They are the framework for the project and its requirements.
- *Follow your approved outline.*
  The outline provides large-scale structural style to guide your work.
- *Use a ring binder.*
  This "modular" approach to physically organizing the first draft makes it easier to handle all that paper.
- *Use tabs.*
  Use tab sheets to mark chapters, appendices, the glossary, the index, and so on. Make it easy for your reviewers to find material.
- *Use a word processor.*
  A word processor or other text-handling program is essential. Remember to make at least two backups of everything and store the backups in different locations.

- *Keep good records.*
  Continue the "audit trail" you began back in the planning stages. As you produce material, *date* each chapter or section and *mark it* with the draft number (for example, Draft 1 – 11/26/90). Many writers like to put this information in a header or footer, because then it shows up on every page.
- *Alert your reviewers that you are starting the first draft.*
  The idea here is to keep everyone aware of the schedule, and let your reviewers know when to expect material for review. In some cases, reviewers may see only part of a manual, depending on their area of specialization and expertise. Plan on calling reviewers often throughout the rest of the project. Don't surprise reviewers by dropping a heap of papers on them with a short review time. Work together to fine-tune the schedule you established in the planning and design stages.

- What is the most efficient way to do a first draft?
- How do you begin writing?
- What about artwork?
- Who sees the first draft?
- What do you do after the first draft has been reviewed?

Fig. 58: First Draft Questions

How Do You Begin Writing?

Since you have an approved outline of the manual, and files of information organized according to that outline, you can begin with any chapter or section.

Some rules of thumb:

- Be sure your information is complete enough to begin writing.
- Review planning and design decisions, and incorporate them into your work.
- Follow agreed-upon manual specifications and page/text formatting, if you are responsible for the appearance of the manual.
- Follow your chapter template to order content properly.
- Pay attention to the principles of good writing.

As you write, make sure your information is complete and accurate. Think of your audience: Given who they are, how can you explain or describe the product so that they find the manual readable, understandable, and usable? How much technical depth should you include? Leave out? What in the audience's background could you use in creating images or making comparisons?

Tip:

If you have trouble writing about something, try to visualize it. Create a mental image of the thing, part, process, service, task, or operation and walk yourself through it. Or take a "hands-on" tour. Make sure you thoroughly understand what you are trying to communicate. If you still have trouble finding the right words, ask yourself whether you need artwork to show the audience what you mean. The right combination of text and artwork is a very powerful teaching tool.

Another method of jogging words loose is to try to teach someone what you are trying to write about. Such interaction can stimulate new ideas or a new way of thinking about the subject. This is especially important when you are still mulling over how to order content and present it to an audience.

Proofread	Proofread for content and language. Edit **content** for accuracy and completeness, given planning and design decisions. Edit **copy** for good writing style, and for elements of craft (grammar, punctuation, spelling, etc.)
Delete	Delete anything that does not serve the purpose of the manual, from entire pages to single words or figures.
Reorder	Reorder content according to mid- and small-scale structural styles in order to make it "flow" more logically. If something seems out of place, move it. Reorganize it.
Revise	Revise your writing until you feel that it reads clearly and logically.

Fig. 59: Editing Your Work

Where's the Action?

Think of the manual as a movie, in that you want to move readers from subject to subject and *show* them what you want them to learn by using action verbs. *Use verbs that show motion* to communicate key issues.

When you show action, don't leave the audience dangling. Psychologically, humans expect "resolution" or "closure" to complete an action. This means that you must present results or draw a conclusion. It is not enough just to see *what* is happening; we want to know *why,* and to find out what happens next.

Editing Your Work

Before you send the "official" first draft to your reviewers, you may have actually edited and revised it several times. After you make an initial stab at getting a chapter or section down on paper, use the above guidelines to improve your work.

What About Artwork?

Use artwork to help present and explain complex aspects of a product. Whether you are working on a large-, mid-, or small-scale (outline, paragraph, or sentence) level, artwork will help you communicate more effectively and quickly by making relationships clear. See *What Is Structural Style?* in chapter 5 for examples of information represented graphically.

User manuals ordinarily contain black-and-white line drawings, diagrams, charts, graphs, text boxes, schematics, tables, and maps. These are commonly referred to as "visuals" or "figures." Tables are sometimes considered to be in a separate "tables" category, and are listed in a list of tables just after the list of figures.

Photographs and illustrations are used less frequently, mostly due to cost of preparation and production.

Several rules of thumb:

- Avoid elaborate artwork.
- Have an in-house or freelance graphic designer handle artwork and page and text formatting, if possible. This will usually ensure higher quality and lower time and cost, as long as the designer is comfortable with the pace and type of work done on the manual. Further, you can probably meet a shorter deadline, since you will be working in parallel.
- Integrate graphics files and text electronically. Most word-processing and computer-based publishing systems accept different types of graphics files. Whenever possible, create and integrate artwork and text on a computer.
- Cut costs by using existing artwork. Scan images into your computer system.
- Modify the complexity and type of figure to suit the audience.

Guidelines

Use the questions in the next figure to analyze your artwork.

There are many reference books on document design. In addition, most computer-based graphics packages now come with clip-art libraries, "template" visuals that can be edited, tutorials, sample page formats, and commonly used figures such as graphs, bars, charts, and so on.

Your objective is to be able to answer "yes" to every question:

- Does every figure have a number and title? Where appropriate, do figures also have captions?
- Do figures show and clarify information in accompanying text?
- Does the text refer to the correct figure?
- Are all figures readable and understandable to your audience?
- Are rows, columns, bars, lines, points, constants, variables, units, measures, symbols, terms, and quantitative scales correct, labeled, and presented accurately? Are they *consistent* with those used in the text?
- If information for figures did *not* come from the product and subject-matter experts, are your sources authoritative? Where appropriate, are sources noted by figures?
- Are your figures clean and uncluttered looking?
- Have you left enough "white space" around each figure, so that the page looks clean and uncluttered?

Fig. 60: Analyzing Your Artwork

Who Sees the First Draft?

Who is on the list of reviewers established during planning and design meetings? The list may include:

- Product experts
- Subject-matter experts
- Project manager
- Content or copy editors
- Art editors
- Marketing or sales personnel
- Legal counsel
- Training and customer-support personnel

If you do not have in-house reviewers, consider the alternatives presented at the beginning of chapter 3.

Help your reviewers help you by letting them know the following:

1. How much time does each reviewer have for review?
2. Which part(s) of the manual is each reviewer supposed to review?
3. What type of critique is each reviewer to give?
   Examples: content
   copy
   artwork
   legal liability
   ... etc.
4. How are reviewers to mark up the text?
   Example:
   Use red ink. Make notes in the left margin.
5. Are reviewers to date and initial the draft itself or a "review log"?
6. Who do reviewers contact if they have questions?

Fig. 61: Guidelines for Reviewing the First Draft

Everyone will not necessarily review the entire manual. If you and the project team have not yet decided who should review what, do this before circulating the first draft. Then, follow these guidelines:

While some companies circulate one copy that everyone sees and marks, others make 30 or more copies and send one to each reviewer. Still others send reviewers only those parts of the manual they are to review. You and the project team must establish a procedure that works for your project. Then, write a memo about the procedure and send it, along with a schedule, to all reviewers.

What Do You Do After the First Draft Has Been Reviewed?

Unless the product changes or you are dealing with reviewers who secretly want to rewrite the text for you, the first draft should be fairly "clean." Why? Because:

- The first draft is the result of careful planning and design by you and the project team.
- You have interviewed product experts to gather information appropriate for the product, audience, and type of manual.
- You have followed an ordered, approved outline and chapter template.
- You have followed the principles of good writing.
- You thought your way through the first draft, selecting appropriate mid- and small-scale structural styles.

After you receive the edited, marked-up first draft from your reviewers:

- *Make revisions* as noted on the first draft.
- *Talk with your experts* if you have any questions.
- *Keep your files updated* with changes, new information, and so on.
- *Begin a "revision file,"* where each draft/revision will be stored until the manual receives final, written approval and is sent into production.

8

AFTER THE FIRST DRAFT: HANDLING REVISIONS

The key to handling revisions is how well you have planned and designed the manual, and how you have handled the first draft. Before you move into the revision stage, you may want to review those chapters, especially chapter 7, as well as the decisions you have made about the project.

How Easily Can You Do Revisions?

If you can answer "yes" to these questions, you should be able to handle revisions quite easily:

- Have you been following your planning and design decisions?
- Have you been following your approved outline?
- Have you been following your approved chapter template?
- Did you follow the principles of good writing in the first draft?
- Have you set up a filing system for information, including updates?
- Have you set up a filing system for each revision (draft) of the manual?

- How easily can you do revisions?
- How do you handle the revision process?

Fig. 62: Revision Issues

Product and subject-matter experts need to check **content** for:

- Accuracy and completeness of text
- Accuracy and completeness of artwork
- Proper use of terms, definitions, units, measures, symbols
- Logical development of subject matter (structural style) in relation to product
- Scope and depth in relation to the audience's background

Fig. 63: Content Editing

- Are you using a computer to handle text and artwork?
- Do you have a review schedule?
- Do your reviewers know who they are and what they have agreed to do?
- Have you kept everyone on the project team informed about all of these issues, by meetings, memos, and phone calls?

Content, Copy, and Art Editing

To help your reviewers do their job, use the checklists shown in figures 63–65. You may want to add more items to each list, but these will get you started.

How Do You Handle the Revision Process?

Coordinating a large, complicated writing project requires careful planning and control. This is particularly true if you do not have a project manager or editor. If you are expected to *manage* the project as well as produce the manual, you have a lot of added responsibility.

Here are some guidelines to help you handle the revision process:

Copy editors need to check **copy** for:

- Principles of good writing style
- Use of the craft of language (spelling, etc.)
- Use of structural styles to develop and communicate content ("flow" and "transition")
- Presentation of product in relation to audience
- Tone (attitude, which is expressed by word choice) in relation to audience
- Pace (speed, or time spent developing and/or explaining a topic) in relation to audience

Fig. 64: Copy Editing

Art editors need to check the **manual** as a whole for:

- Page and text formatting in relation to:
    audience
    type of manual
    how the manual will be used
- Consistency of formatting throughout the manual
- Coordination of text and artwork

Fig. 65: Art Editing

Deadline

When is the deadline?

This is the first issue to address and fine-tune, as it may have changed one or more times since your initial planning and design meetings. First, ask these questions:

- When are published copies to be ready for distribution?
- When are approved, original pages to be ready to go to press?

Then, work backward from the due date(s) to establish a schedule for each stage of the revision process:

- Modifying the outline, due to product modifications
- Gathering updated information
- Rewriting and proofreading
- Reviewing and editing content, copy, and artwork

What has to be done?
By whom?
When?
Be sure that everyone gets a copy of schedules and deadlines.
Put everything in writing.
Set up a system so that you are told about changes to the product.
Take the initiative and stay in touch with all reviewers.

Reviews

Review after each revision. Since you are working on a computer, you and the reviewers will only have to check those portions of the manual that have been changed.

Keep good language reference texts on hand for questions about craft.

Keep your outline handy and follow it.

Call the experts if you have questions about updated content.

When you send reviewers a new draft to review and edit, send along the previous, marked-up draft. Don't make them guess where you or they made changes—they won't remember without hard copy.

Some word-processing software contains "redline" or "document comparison" options, which you may prefer to use, instead of making copies of the previous draft.

Approvals

Have reviewers date and initial each revision.

Get written approval on final copy and artwork.

Audit Trail

Save everything!

Date and number all revisions!

Always leave a paper or computer-based trail!

The revision process can take a long time, especially if the product is modified. You must keep track of which changes have been made in order to make editing easier for your reviewers and yourself. You may also need the audit trail to verify what you have done, or to check on why a change was made, say 11 revisions ago, if someone questions you about your work.

Save *all* drafts and revisions of *text and artwork* until *after* the final, original pages of the manual have received written approval, *and* copies have been produced.

9

EVALUATING YOUR MANUAL

Use this chapter to help *control the process* of creating a manual and ensure that the final document meets planning, design, and project requirements.

You can evaluate a manual only if you have a standard, or "yardstick," against which to measure results. Therefore, to successfully evaluate what you have written, you must have planning and design decisions available for comparison.

What Are Some Common Problems In Writing?

Bad Planning and Design

Lack of proper planning and design is indicated by the following:

- *Users feel left out.*
  The manual is written in technobabble, understandable only to those in the know. Users feel "talked at" or "talked down to," instead of having concepts, procedures, and terms explained and taught in a clear, simple way. Successful manuals (and products!) take the audience into account.
- *Users feel as though they aren't "going anywhere" when they read the manual.*
  This often occurs when the writer hasn't created or followed an outline, and users become entangled in unclear writing. Without a large-scale structural style, the manual will ramble along in a disorganized, fragmented way. Without proper use of mid- and small-scale struc-

tural styles, there will be no sense of flow, transition, or development of the subject matter.

- *Users can't find information.*
  Many manuals have only a minimal table of contents. Many lack a list of figures, list of tables, or an index. Without these "pointers," users are forced to deal with the manual as though it were a novel, to be read from beginning to end. This is not a useful way to read a manual.
- *Users feel pushed away from the page.*
  Lack of headers, footers, and other elements of page and text formatting force users to work much harder than they should have to. By contrast, visual clarity aids understanding and learning.

- What are some common problems in writing?
- Is the manual usable?
- Did you sequence material properly?
- What did you say?
- When is the manual finished?

Fig. 66: Evaluation Issues

Bad Information

This problem is usually caused by bad planning and design. Read the chapters on planning, design, and information gathering again, and you will see what I mean. Information problems are indicated by the following:

- *Users feel that there is too much "extra" information.*
- *Users feel that there is too little information.*
- *Users feel that the information is too technical or too basic.*
- *Users find that the product information is incorrect.*

In order to answer the question "*What* am I going to say in this manual?," you must know your product, its purpose, your audience, what type of manual you are writing, and how the manual is to be used, for example. The answers to planning and design questions guide information gathering.

Bad Writing

This problem is caused mostly by poor craft (spelling, grammar, etc.) or a writing style that is not appropriate for a manual, and is indicated by the following:

- *Users cannot understand what you are trying to communicate, due to your use of language.*
  Bad grammar, incorrect spelling, and misuse of punctuation are common culprits.
- *Users are confused, because you refer to one item in many different ways.*
  Remember to be consistent in use of terms, definitions, and so on.
- *Users get tangled in long, convoluted sentences and overcomplicated expressions.*
  Analyze your language for wordiness, clichés, and bad elements of craft, such as grammar and syntax. Get to the point. Keep your paragraphs, sentences, and words short and simple.
- *Users cannot understand made-up verbs or phrases.*
  Do not create "illegal" verbs. You cannot just turn nouns into verbs, or add "-ize" to perfectly nice nouns and verbs. Check your dictionary. Also, avoid gobbledygook; write "pencil," not "portable hand-held communications inscriber," as some in the military do, according to William Lutz, editor of the *Quarterly Review of Doublespeak.* Use language to communicate, not to hide.

Refer to chapter 6 for more help in analyzing your work.

Is the Manual Usable?

Use the following checklist to catch the most common problems.

Outline

First, check overall organization. Have you followed your outline? Is the structural style appropriate, given the product, its purpose, your audi-

```
Outline
Introduction or preface
Titles and headings
Balance
Error messages
Exercises or applications
Pointers
Figures
Formatting
```

Fig. 67: Usability Checklist

ence, the type of manual you are writing, and how the manual is to be used?

Read the table of contents. It is your most visible "road map." What does it tell you?

If you followed your outline, the table of contents should give you a sense of "seeing" the entire manual, of grasping the whole. Reviewers and testers should get the same impression.

Introduction or Preface

The introduction or preface should answer these questions:

- What is the purpose of the product?
- What is the purpose of the manual?
- Who is the audience?
- How is the manual organized?
- How should the audience use the manual?
- Are any other customer-support services available?

Titles and Headings

Read the first paragraph under each chapter or section title or heading. Will it help users keep their bearings? Does it show the logical order (structural style) of material? Are objectives and purpose explicitly stated?

Balance

Do you balance concepts and procedures—the "why" and the "how"? Are they in proper proportion for the type of manual you are writing?

Error Messages

Does the manual contain a chapter or section on error messages? Is each error message fully explained? Does each error message contain a diagnostic (probable causes) and tell users how to correct the error condition?

Exercises or Applications

Does the manual show users how to apply the product to solving problems? Tasks geared to specific problem-solving objectives help users learn.

Pointers

Does the manual help users find information? Is there a detailed table of contents? A list of figures? A list of tables? An index? Appendices for important but seldom-used information?

Figures

Check all figures. Do they support the text? Will users know when they are supposed to refer to them? Are they clearly labeled, with sources noted where appropriate? Does each figure have a specific purpose?

Formatting

Is your text readable? Are you using elements of page and text formatting? Are your pages well-formatted and inviting, or crowded and messy?

- Is everything where it should be?
- Do you proceed from the general to the specific?
- Do you cross-reference where necessary?
- Does it all hang together?

Fig. 68: Sequencing Checklist

Did You Sequence Material Properly?

If the large-scale (outline), mid-scale (paragraph), and small-scale (sentence) structural styles of your manual prevent users from easily learning about the product and how to use it to get a job done, then the manual will not communicate. It will not be usable or effective. Your work will not meet project requirements.

When you are in the thick of writing and revising, how can you keep yourself organized in order to reach project goals? How can you judge whether you are handling information properly, from the "big picture" down to the details?

Is Everything Where It Should Be?

How do you find out?

First, is the manual organized according to the outline?

Second, can a tester use the manual to solve a problem or get a job done?

Do You Proceed from the General to the Specific?

Does the manual present an overview of the product and the manual itself?

Do you show the "big picture"?

Do you present each part of the "big picture" in detail?

Do You Cross-Reference Where Necessary?

Does the manual contain a cross-referenced index?
Do you cross-reference in the text, where appropriate?

Examples of when to cross-reference in text:

- The manual contains a lot of repetitious material.
- Many branches of a program call or are called by the same menus, procedures, functions, or commands.

Does It All Hang Together?

Read the manual after you think it is finished. As you read, do you feel that you get to know the product? Do you understand how to use it to get a job done?

Now ask someone else to read the manual and answer those questions.

- Does anything in the manual puzzle me?
- Does everything in the manual have a purpose?
- Does the manual read well—is the content continuous and coherent?
- Can I move easily from a conceptual understanding of the product to its applications (from the general to the specific)?

Fig. 69: Can I Understand the Manual?

Skim the manual and check the following:	Ask yourself these questions:
Where's the action?	Where are the "action" verbs? Do they show users what to do?
Where does the action change?	How will users spot a difference, contradiction, or exception? Are these changes signaled by "similarity/difference" words? **Examples:** although yet nevertheless despite but however even though rather except
Where is the action summarized?	How will users spot a summary or repetition that could be skipped once they learn about the product? Are these changes signaled by "summary" words? **Examples:** in summary in addition and also moreover and too furthermore more besides
Where does the action draw to a close?	How will users spot a conclusion? Are these changes signaled by "cause/effect" words? **Examples:** therefore consequently in conclusion as a result accordingly so
How is the action highlighted?	Do page and text formatting set off the action by grabbing users' attention?

Fig. 70: Skimming for Comprehension

What Did You Say?

Review the manual. As you read, refer to your planning and design decisions, product information files, and the principles of good writing. Ask yourself the questions listed in figure 70.

Then, skim the manual.

Reviewers

After you have marked potential problem areas, have your reviewers check the manual.

Almost-Final Questions

If, after all reviews and revisions have been made, you can answer "yes" to the questions listed in figure 71, then you have probably said what you intended to say.

- Does the table of contents reflect the outline?
- Does each chapter/section follow the chapter template?
- Is technical content accurate and complete?
- Is information presented concisely?
- Do you take your audience into account?
- Have you followed the principles of good writing?
- Are your text and artwork coordinated?

Fig. 71: Almost-Final Questions

When Is the Manual Finished?

The questions in figure 72 bring you to the end of the evaluation process. Use them to help decide whether the manual is finished and ready for production.

- Have the experts told you the product is "frozen"? This means that there will be no further changes in the current release that affect the manual.
- Have you followed an approved outline?
- Have product and subject-matter experts given written approval to all facts, procedures, operations, and tasks?
- Do you have final, written approval?
- To the best of your ability, is the manual clear?
- Have you used the principles of good writing to analyze and improve your writing in the manual?
- Does your tone indicate that your attitude toward users is sincere and respectful?
- Are your sentences varied in length? Does every sentence, word, and figure have a purpose?
- Are page and text formatting inviting? Do your pages draw readers' attention?
- Are your text and artwork flawless? No smudges or misalignments?

Fig. 72: The Finish Line

10

PRODUCTION

During production, copies of the original, camera-ready pages of the manual are produced for distribution to customers.

Since most manuals are copied or printed onto paper, this chapter gives guidelines for the production of paper manuals.

Who Belongs on the Support Team?

What assistance do you need? It all depends on how the manual is to be produced. This chapter addresses the production of a manual on paper.

Do you need a graphic designer/illustrator for cover art?

Do you need a supplier of ring binders or diecut tabs?

Do you need a typesetter?

Do you need a production artist for pasteup?

Will you need a copy shop or a printer?

Are you responsible for coordinating everyone and the schedule?

- Who belongs on the support team?
- How will you produce the original pages?
- How is the manual to be produced?

Fig. 73: Production Issues

Text (hard copy on paper)
Video
Online
Audio
Computer-based training
Optical disk
Diskettes
Interactive videodisc
Microfiche
Hypertext
CD ROM

Fig. 74: Production Media

Get Expert Help

Get expert help, especially if you have little experience in producing printed material. This is particularly important when:

- Many copies are to be produced.
- The shipping schedule is complex.
- The manual's production specifications are complex.

A professional printer, production editor, copy shop manager, or graphic designer knows the production business and understands the importance of meeting a production schedule.

If you are expected to handle production scheduling and coordination, throw yourself on the mercy of someone at your copy shop or printer:

- Ask what is expected of you.
- Ask what you must supply.
- Ask how jobs are scheduled.
- Ask for guidance throughout production.

Be sure to tell your contact at the copy shop or printer that you have very little experience. Keep in close touch.

How Will You Produce the Original Pages?

Are you working on a computer-based publishing system? Are you to specify typefaces and handle page and text formatting? Or, will you need a typesetter and a graphic designer?

More and more, text and art are integrated on computer systems, and the original, camera-ready pages are printed on a laser printer. You may handle this yourself, or send disks to someone in-house or outside.

Allow time to print out original pages!

Laser printers, especially Postscript type, can require up to several minutes to print a large figure. For several hundred pages of text with 150 figures or so, allow at least one week.

Checking Original Pages

Follow these guidelines:

- Proofread originals for print quality.
- Collate in correct page order.
- Insert any pasted-up pages into the original set.
- Touch up any artwork as necessary.
- Place a copy of the production specs on top of the originals. Mark in red that this sheet is to be removed before running the job.
- Get dated approval in writing of the set of originals, and file it.
- Proofread the originals once again, looking closely at page order.
- Wrap and box the originals for protection during delivery to the production house.
- Label the box containing the originals:
  Title of manual
  Date
  Number of original pages
  Your name, company name, and phone
  Due date for copies
  Name of your contact at the copy shop or printer
  Note that production specs are inside the box

How Is the Manual to Be Produced?

Get Bids on Copying or Printing

In design meetings, you and the project team decided whether the manual was to be produced on a copier or a printing press. Based on the manual's specifications, you should already have gotten several bids *in writing* for the job. Be sure to get cost *and* time bids.

Remember that the lowest bid may reflect lower quality and service. For high-quality results, you must take creativity and professionalism into account.

Communicate with the Production People

Do *not* surprise the folks in production with a last-minute schedule change, a "little" additional material, or anything else. Such things can significantly alter the production specifications, cost, and time required for your job.

Be sure that the copy shop or printer knows the deadline!

Be sure you schedule production from two to six months (or more) before deadline, depending on the size of the job!

Use Originals

Give the production people original pages, artwork (mechanicals), and photographs (negatives or transparencies). Do not use copies; they will not reproduce well.

Ask for a Press Proof

If you are producing many copies, or if you are working with a new production house, ask for a *press proof*.

A press proof is a single copy of the reproduced manual that lets you check paper, ink, photo, and gray-shade or color quality, *before* 50,000 of them roll off the production line.

The press proof is a semifinal Quality Assurance/Quality Control (QA/QC) check.

After Production

Open a few cartons and check the shrink-wrapping. Is it too tight? Too loose? Open a few manuals and thumb through them to check production quality:

Are text and art horizontal or crooked?

Are they placed too far left or right?

Does print quality look good or bad?

Are ring binder holes smoothly drilled?

If you spot any problems, call the production house. Have a decision-maker meet you at your office to look over the problems and decide how they will be resolved.

This is your final QA/QC check.

Now it's your customers' turn.

11

EXERCISES

Think your way through each exercise by using the planning and design lists of questions, creating an outline, gathering details, and applying the principles of good writing to your work.

If you do these exercises with a group, and assign each member a "project team" role to play, you should be able to simulate the entire writing process, from planning to evaluation.

1. Pretend that someone who has never seen or used a coat has asked you to describe one: What is a coat? What does it do? Why would you use one? How is it used?

What do you have to know about your audience? How do you describe a coat and its uses *simply*—but *not simplistically?* How can you make your description clear, complete, and concise, yet avoid underwriting, which will make your work unclear and incomplete?

2. Define the word "chair." How is a chair different from a bench or a sofa? What are the essential qualities of "chair-ness"? How did chairs evolve? What is their history? Why do some cultures lack chairs? Why are there so many types of chair?

Your objective in defining something is to create a perception in the mind of the reader that matches your own.

3. This exercise will give you practice in solving some of the problems that seminar attendees bring up in class for discussion:

If you have to use a poorly written or outdated manual in your job, what can you do about it? Or, what if you have discovered that some product (that is, any procedure, thing, service, or program) in your company needs to be effectively explained?

Use the techniques presented in this book to analyze the problem and solve it by writing a good user manual. If the project is too large, talk with your boss about how to make room for it in your work schedule.

If you intend to rewrite a poorly written manual, first use chapter 9 to analyze the manual's strengths and weaknesses and establish standards for the new manual.

4. Imagine you are in history class, studying the Constitution of the United States. Your assignment is to write a manual that describes the organization of the government, including the qualifications and powers of federal officers. Even though the Cabinet and other independent offices are extraconstitutional bodies, your professor wants you to include them as well.

As you know, our government is composed of the executive, legislative, and judicial branches. They are supposed to have equal power.

The legislative branch, for example, comprises the Congress, the General Accounting Office, the Government Printing Office, and the Library of Congress, among others. What parts make up the executive and judicial branches?

How many Cabinet members and independent offices are there? To which branch do they report?

If you are working on your own, do one of the following: skip those planning and design questions meant for a project team, answer them all yourself, or ask an expert those questions.

For this exercise, your best resources will probably be the library (see your friendly reference librarian), a bookstore, or a government publication office.

5. Create an outline for a book about wildflowers in your region. Find a local botanist with knowledge of wildflowers for product interviews. You may need to take a "hands-on" tour and go on field trips.

Who is the audience? How will they use your book? How much scientific detail must you include (for example, descriptions, flowering dates, habitat, range, history, and related families)? Will drawings suffice, or are full-color photographs required?

What are the parts of a flower? When is a flower a wildflower, as opposed to a garden variety? How do you tell a wildflower from a weed? Which wildflowers are also classified as herbs? Which wildflowers can be cultivated? How are wildflower families and species classified? Should your book contain a section that groups flowers by color, for easy identification by lay readers?

6. Describe a hard disk drive. Try using comparisons. Don't use jargon. What is a hard disk? Why do computers have them? What do hard disks do? Why do computer users prefer hard disks to diskettes, especially for large projects?

7. Define RAM for someone who knows nothing about computers. What is RAM? Why do computers have it? How does RAM differ from other storage media, such as diskettes or a hard disk? How is it used?

8. Pretend that you work for a cutlery firm and have been asked to write a small manual about sharpening knives. A manual is packaged with each set of knives.

Here, your real product is not the knife, but care of the knife, specifically the process of sharpening it. What do you know about this? Where could you find information? What are the basic steps in the process?

Who is your audience? When would they need to sharpen a knife? Does your company sell sharpeners? What visuals (artwork) would help explain this process, while stressing safety and decreasing the likelihood of an accident?

It might be interesting to pretend that you have been bitten by the entrepreneurial bug and now feel driven to start a cutlery-manufacturing business. Use some of the resources suggested in this book at the beginning of chapter 3, as well as library research, government publications, and information interviews with outside experts to create your manual.

9. Every car is delivered with an owner's manual. In this exercise, write an outline for such a manual. For more extensive practice, select one or two chapters in your outline and write at least a first draft.

Unless you have contacts in the automotive-manufacturing industry, your local car dealer or mechanic would make a good product expert. Since they also get a lot of first-hand customer feedback, they may be able to offer valuable suggestions on content for your audience.

How do you start to break the whole car (system) down into major subdivisions (sets) and, finally, components (parts)? Major subdivisions might include, for example, the body, various controls, the engine, and the fuel and exhaust subsystems.

After you have done this, consider your audience and the type of manual you are writing to help yourself decide which order to select for the outline.

10. Let's say that you have been asked to write a manual to standardize operating procedures for accounts receivable (A/R). If this is a new field for you, find a product expert for interviews, perhaps someone in your company, or a friend who works in this area.

Focus on:

- Writing directions to standardize the actions of A/R staff.
- Showing staff how to use the product so that A/R runs the way management wants it to. (In this case, the product is a group of procedures.)
- Explaining each procedure and how they all fit together.

What do you need to find out about the daily balance? Exception reports? Handling errors? What about cash applications, including check batches and customer deductions? Do you need to include information on execution of wire transfers, daily deduction tracking, and document storage? How is deduction processing handled?

What else should be included?

INDEX